The Soviet Union Under Gorbachev

Assessing the First Year

Edited by
Arthur B. Gunlicks
and
John D. Treadway

PRAEGER

New York
Westport, Connecticut
London

Library of Congress Cataloging-in-Publication Data

The Soviet Union under Gorbachev-assessing the first year.

Includes index.
1. Soviet Union—Politics and government—
1953–   . 2. Soviet Union—Social conditions—
1970–   . 3. Soviet Union—Economic conditions—
1976–   . 4. Soviet Union—Foreign relations—
1975–   . 5. Gorbachev, Mikhail Sergeevich,
1931–   . I. Gunlicks, Arthur B., 1936–   .
II. Treadway, John D.
DK286.15.S694   1987   947.085'4   87-7002
ISBN 0-275-92701-6 (alk. paper)
ISBN 0-275-92702-4 (pbk: alk. paper)

Copyright © 1987 by Arthur B. Gunlicks and John D. Treadway

All rights reserved. No portion of this book may be reproduced, by any process or technique, without the express written consent of the publisher.

Library of Congress Catalog Card Number: 87-7002
ISBN: 0-275-92701-6 (hb)
       0-275-92702-4 (pbk)

First published in 1987

Praeger Publishers, One Madison Avenue, New York, NY 10010
A division of Greenwood Press, Inc.

Printed in the United States of America

The paper used in this book complies with the Permanent Paper Standard issued by the National Information Standards Organization (Z39.48-1984).

10 9 8 7 6 5 4 3 2 1

Contents

Figures		vii
Preface		ix
1	Gorbachev, the Party, and the Soviet State Arthur B. Gunlicks	1
2	Gorbachev's First Year: An Overview Helmut Sonnenfeldt	17
3	The Gorbachev Generation Konstantin Simis	33
4	Soviet Foreign Policy Under Gorbachev: Goals and Expectations Dimitri K. Simes	55
5	Gorbachev's Economic Prescriptions: A Preliminary Analysis John P. Hardt and Jean Farneth Boone	73
6	Social Policy Under Gorbachev Walter D. Connor	95
7	Soviet Culture: New Attitudes Toward the Arts Irwin Weil	121

8	Gorbachev and the 27th Party Congress of the CPSU J. Martin Ryle	137

Recommended Readings 151
Index 153
About the Editors and Contributors 161

Figures

1 Structure of the Communist Party of the Soviet Union   7
2 Structure of the Soviet State   11

Preface

During the first half of the 1980s, the world witnessed a rapid succession of Soviet leaders, from Brezhnev to Andropov to Chernenko, and finally, to Gorbachev. But when Mikhail Gorbachev became general secretary of the Communist party of the Soviet Union, it was obvious that barring an unexpected illness or accident, this new Soviet leader would probably be at the helm of the Soviet state for a long time, perhaps into the next century. His relative youthfulness, energy, and apparent openness to new ideas and policies led many students of Soviet politics to believe that Gorbachev might bring about significant changes in Soviet domestic policies as well as in the conduct of foreign affairs.

In order to provide the broader university and metropolitan community with an assessment of the new leader and some informed speculation about the future of Soviet–U.S. relations, Professor Joseph Troncale, director of the Russian Studies program at the University of Richmond, organized and obtained the funding for a symposium in late January and early February 1986 consisting of a number of well-known Soviet scholars. Following the symposium, we accepted editorial responsibility for putting together manuscripts based in part on the presentations at the symposium, to be included in a collection of essays that focus on Gorbachev's first year in office. The chapters by Helmut Sonnenfeldt, Konstantin Simis, Dimitri Simes, John Hardt and J. F. Boone, and Irwin Weil are based on the authors' presentations made at the Richmond symposium. Some of these chapters have been revised and updated to reflect developments at the 27th Party Congress, held a month after the symposium. The chapter by Arthur Gunlicks was added as an introduction, the chapter by Walter Connor was included because of the relevance of the subject matter, and the chapter on the Party Congress, by Martin Ryle, was added as a conclusion that would focus on this major event at the end of Gorbachev's first year in power.

We wish to thank Professor Troncale for his assistance in the preparation of this book; the staff members of the Learning Resources Center at the University of Richmond for their services; and Dean Sheldon Wettack for the financial and institutional support he was able to provide at a number of stages.

Arthur B. Gunlicks
John D. Treadway

The Soviet Union
Under Gorbachev

1 Gorbachev, the Party, and the Soviet State
Arthur B. Gunlicks

Arthur Gunlicks' introductory chapter lays the groundwork for the chapters that follow. First he scrutinizes the myth and reality of what some might term the "youth movement" in the Soviet leadership. Next he provides a short primer on the Soviet political system, distinguishing between "party" and "state," while clarifying their unique interrelationship in the Soviet system. In the section on "Gorbachev and the Party," Gunlicks introduces the reader to the basic institutions of the Communist party hierarchy, such as the Politburo, Secretariat, and All Union Party Congress. He then details some of the personnel changes that have taken place in the party under Gorbachev's leadership. In the following section he similarly explains the fundamental organs of government (the state) and the leadership changes that have taken place in the past year. What do the extraordinary personnel changes of the past year portend, if anything? For all the authors in this book the guiding question is whether Gorbachev's selection as general secretary of the Communist Party of the Soviet Union (CPSU) heralds a new era in Soviet history or simply "more of the same."

THE LEADERSHIP TRANSITION

When Mikhail Gorbachev assumed power on March 11, 1985, he became the fourth Soviet leader in less than three years. His immediate predecessor, Konstantin Chernenko, had served less than thirteen months. Chernenko's predecessor, Yuri Andropov, had led the Soviet Union for only fifteen months, at least six of which he was ill. Andropov's predecessor, Leonid Brezhnev, had also been ailing for several years before he died in November 1982.

It is not surprising, then, that by 1985 a picture of Soviet leaders had emerged that suggested a feeble, tired, conservative, and dull gerontocracy. In contrast Gorbachev, 54 and apparently in excellent health, seemed to be unusually young, dynamic, and energetic. During their visit to London in December 1984, the Western press even began comparing him and his wife, Raisa, an attractive and stylish woman, to John and Jackie Kennedy.

The perception that Gorbachev's assumption of power represented a striking shift toward youth and stability is doubly ironic. First, the leadership instability of the 1980s stood in sharp contrast to the norms of Soviet history. In the 65 years between 1917 and 1982, only four men exercised supreme power in the Soviet Union: Lenin for five years, until 1922 (he was ill from the fall of 1922 to his death in January 1924); Stalin for a quarter of a century, from the mid-to-late 1920s until March 1953; Khrushchev, for eleven years, from an uncertain beginning in the fall of 1953 until October 1964; and Brezhnev for eighteen years, from 1964 until November 1982. During the same 65-year period thirteen presidents, from Woodrow Wilson to Ronald Reagan, served in the United States.

The contrast between Gorbachev's youth and the gerontocracy he replaced offers the second irony. Most of the first Soviet leaders were relatively young men, not surprising considering that they were newly successful revolutionaries; and until the 1970s few members of the Soviet elite could be characterized as old. When Stalin succeeded Lenin, he (and Trotsky) were, at 44, among the oldest members of the ruling elite. Khrushchev was 59 when he became the Soviet leader, Brezhnev 57. It was Brezhnev's age (76) at his death, the average age of his colleagues in the Politburo (68), and the ages of Andropov and Chernenko (68 and 72, respectively) when they assumed power that made Gorbachev look so very young. One might add that the advanced ages of most other ruling communist leaders in China, North Korea, Vietnam, and Eastern Europe contributed to Gorbachev's youthful impression. While Gorbachev was only a few years younger than Brezhnev and Khrushchev were when they assumed power, he still differed from them in that he was relatively younger than his colleagues in the Soviet elite.[1]

Of greater importance than his age, perhaps, is that Gorbachev represents a new generation of leadership. He began his career in 1955, two years after Stalin's death, and therefore cannot be implicated in Stalin's terror. Indeed, Gorbachev and the new leaders he has brought into elite positions have been critical of the past leadership, even though they have benefited from and support the political and economic system they have inherited and which they hope to improve and revitalize but not necessarily change in any dramatic way. Gorbachev is also better educated than his predecessors, having studied law at Moscow State University in the 1950s and received a degree in agricultural economics in 1967.

In spite of the differences between Gorbachev and his predecessors, he was, like all of them at the time they assumed power, a full member of the Politburo and a secretary of the Central Committee of the Communist Party. The only other man who shared these qualifications at the time of Chernenko's death was Grigori Romanov, the head of the Leningrad party organization. Considered a serious rival to Gorbachev, Romanov disappeared from public view several weeks after Gorbachev took command of the party; he announced his retirement from the Politburo "for reasons of health" on July 1, 1985.

PARTY AND STATE

In any discussion of leadership in the Soviet Union and in other communist countries, it is necessary to distinguish between party leadership on the one hand and the leading positions of the state or government on the other (Europeans refer to "the state" in much the same way Americans talk about "the government"). While in virtually all modern, industrialized countries, party leaders control the institutions of the state, there are crucial differences between the Western democracies and the Communist systems in the nature and extent of "party rule." In the democratic countries there are, by definition, two or more parties that compete in open electoral contests for power. In countries with parliamentary systems, usually the majority party or majority coalition of parties in the legislature forms a government, the leader of which, generally called the prime minister, is the majority party leader (e.g., Great Britain) or a party leader in the coalition government (e.g., virtually every country on the Western European continent). While there is a degree of cohesion and discipline in these parties that is generally lacking in the United States, the party leaders must nevertheless satisfy various wings, factions, or groups in the party in order to maintain credibility and unity. They cannot dictate to their parties, at least not in the long run. But both party leaders and their followers recognize that party unity is the prerequisite for strong, effective, and stable government, due to the dependence of the government on continuing majority support in the parliamentary assembly. In the United States, with its separately elected president, House of Representatives, and Senate, and with its loosely organized, fragmented, and poorly disciplined parties, a direct, consistent, and meaningful relationship between party and government leadership may be difficult to find. Indeed, it may be only a slight exaggeration to speak of a "no-party" system rather than of a two-party system in the United States.

The highly disciplined Communist Party of the Soviet Union (CPSU) is at the opposite end of the continuum from the highly individualistic parties in the United States. The CPSU is also a considerable distance from the strongly disciplined Western European parties, which occupy a middle position. One important difference between the Communist party of the Soviet Union and most Western parties is, of course, that there is only one party in the Soviet Union. A second difference is that organized factions and wings are not tolerated, so that at least to the outside observer there is an impression of complete unity. A third difference is that a small party elite, located in the Politburo, determines party policy, frequently without having to consider the views of lower party organs. A fourth difference is the theory and practice of party supremacy over state (or government) institutions. Thus judicial independence is limited, especially in cases of political importance. Lack of legislative independence is demonstrated by the fact that the Supreme Soviet, the country's nominal parliament, meets for only a few days each year and passes all laws and resolutions by unanimous vote. In important matters not even executive independence exists, since the party, through the Secretariat of the Central Committee, supervises the implementation of all important state activities. This includes not only the ministries but also industrial and agricultural production in the state-owned factories and farms.

Gorbachev and the Party

Gorbachev's power is derived from his position as general secretary (called first secretary under Khrushchev) of the Communist Party of the Soviet Union (see Figure 1). As general secretary he not only heads the Secretariat of the Central Committee, but he also presides over the Politburo.

The Politburo (called Presidium under Khrushschev), which meets about once a week, is the major policymaking body of the party. It consists of about a dozen full members (and six to eight candidate members—usually somewhat younger men who are next in line for full membership and until then do not have a vote), some of whom, like the general secretary, are also members of the Secretariat and are therefore even more powerful. Others may be leaders of institutions of the state, such as the prime minister (Chairman of the Council of Ministers), foreign minister, head of the secret police (KGB), or heads of other major ministries or organizations. All are members of the Central Committee, which elects the Politburo and the secretaries of the Secretariat.

The Secretariat is the party's administrative nerve center, its means of supervising and therefore controlling the state bureaucracy, including the military and secret police. It is organized into about two dozen departments which are rather similar to the departments one would expect to find in a government cabinet. For the USSR this means a certain correspondence between the departments of the party's Secretariat and the state ministries in the Council of Ministers described below. The department heads of the Secretariat include the eleven secretaries plus the general secretary who is also the party leader. Given the intrusiveness and omnipresence of the state in Soviet society and a barely existent private sector, the supervision by the *party* bureaucracy (namely, the Secretariat) over the ubiquitous and bloated *state* bureaucracy is a crucial device of party rule. The Party Control Committee, also shown in Figure 1, is concerned with issues of party discipline and is charged with carrying out the occasional purges of the party membership.

The Secretariat is also of central importance for the party itself; whoever controls the Secretariat is in a position to control the party apparatus from the top down. This means that to assure that his supporters are elected to the Politburo and Secretariat, the general secretary must control the membership of the Central Committee, a body composed of approximately 300 (307 in 1986) full members and about 150 candidate members. These individuals represent the top officials of the Communist party, the government, the military, and scientific, educational, and cultural organizations. The Central Committee meets about every six months and is charged officially with carrying out the wishes of the party on behalf of the Party Congress, which elects the Central Committee.

The All-Union Party Congress consists of about 5,000 delegates and meets once every five years, most recently in February–March 1986. Essentially a rubber stamp for the party leadership, it is nevertheless important for the Politburo to exercise some control over delegate selection. This was especially the case in the early years after the Bolshevik revolution, when issues were debated and leaders were challenged. The fact that Stalin occupied the position of general secretary after Lenin's death gave him the opportunity to gain control over the party bureaucracy and over selection of delegates to the All-Union Party Congress. This, in turn, enabled him to weaken and then eliminate all real and potential rivals in the party. Later, the appointment of Khrushchev as general secretary also made it

Figure 1 Structure of the Communist Party of the Soviet Union

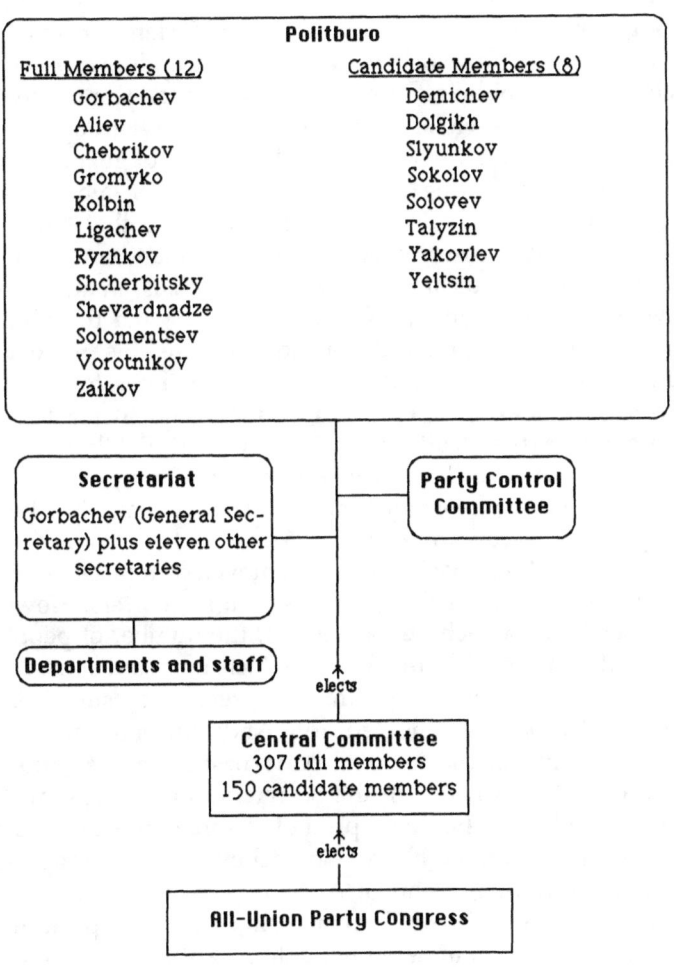

possible for him to outmaneuver his rivals and gain undisputed control over the party by 1957.

A kind of patronage politics, then, is required of any leader who becomes general secretary and wants to retain his position. But the example of Khrushchev demonstrates that although patronage is necessary, it is not sufficient for remaining in office. While Khrushchev had seen his friends and associates elected to the Politburo, Secretariat and Central Committee, especially after his victory over the "anti-party group" in the summer of 1957, his actions and policies did not guarantee continued support among all his appointees. His famous secret speech in which he denounced Stalin before the 20th Party Congress in 1956 contributed to unrest in Poland and Hungary and raised questions among Soviet intellectuals. In addition his adventurous deployment of missiles in Cuba and their humiliating withdrawal under American pressure; his removal of numerous lower level party officials, sometimes for arbitrary reasons; and his mercurial temperament and increasing susceptibility to the "cult of personality" led Politburo and/or Secretariat members Brezhnev, Kosygin, Podgorny, Suslov, and Shelepin to conspire against him and replace him while he was away from Moscow in October 1964.[2]

As expected, Gorbachev has also moved to replace older and less reliable party officials with his own supporters. However, the speed with which he has moved, the number of people he has replaced, and the manner in which he has dismissed numerous officials have caught many observers by surprise. It is true that Gorbachev benefited from Andropov's replacement of about one-fifth of the regional party first secretaries and nine of 23 department heads in the Secretariat of the Central Committee. Andropov had also promoted three men to candidate membership in the Politburo; Gorbachev moved quickly on his own and toward the end of April 1985 he elevated the three candidate members to full membership.[3] By late spring it was clear that he had eliminated his only potential rival, Romanov, who then announced his retirement on July 1; the following day Andrei Gromyko, the Soviet Union's foreign minister since 1957, became the "president" (see below) of the Soviet Union and a full member of the Politburo. Eduard Shevardnadze, also a full member of the Politburo, replaced him as foreign minister. On September 27 Gorbachev replaced Nikolai Tikhonov, the aging prime minister (see Figure 2), with Nikolai Ryzhkov. In March 1986, at the end of the 27th Party Congress, Lev Zaikov was named to full membership in the Politburo, while two octogenarian Brezhnev appointees were retired. At the same time five new party secretaries were named to the Secretariat, including Anatoly Dobrynin, who had served as Soviet ambassador to the United States for a quarter of a century, and Aleksandra Birynkov, the first woman in a key leadership position since 1961.[4] By the end of the party congress, Gorbachev had appointed or promoted five full members to the Politburo and five candidate members. He had also named seven of the eleven party secretaries in the Secretariat. Besides himself, only two secretaries were also full members of the Politburo: Ligachev and Zaikov. At least 119 full members of the Central Committee were his appointees as well.

Gorbachev and the State

Just as the All-Union Party Congress is supposed to be the highest organ of the party, the Supreme Soviet, the legislative body of the Soviet Union, is, according to the Soviet constitution, "the highest body of state authority." In fact, as indicated above, it is little more than a rubber stamp for party and government leaders.

The Supreme Soviet consists of two houses, the Soviet of the Union and the Soviet of Nationalities (see Figure 2). The Soviet of the Union is roughly comparable to the U.S. House of Representatives in that it represents the Soviet people as a whole. Unlike the U.S. Senate, however, which represents the fifty states, the Soviet of Nationalities does not represent the fifteen Soviet republics. Rather, it is the representative body for the approximately one hundred officially recognized national or ethnic groups that comprise the Soviet population. Each house has about 750 deputies, elected in districts of equal population (Soviet of the Union) or in areas occupied by the different ethnic or language groups (Soviet of Nationalities). The Supreme Soviet meets only twice a year for a few days each time.

Because of its infrequent and brief meetings, the Supreme Soviet elects a Presidium to act in its place when it is not in session. The Presidium consists of thirty-nine members, fifteen of whom are the chairmen of the republics' supreme soviets (roughly comparable to U.S. state legislatures). The Presidium has a number of important legislative functions, including the issuance of decrees with the force of law when the Supreme Soviet is not in session. While these are supposed to be ratified later by the Supreme Soviet, the more sensitive decrees may be withheld from legislative "scrutiny." The other decrees that are presented to the Supreme Soviet are approved routinely by that body when it does meet. The Presidium also has a number of executive functions, the best known of which is serving as a collective head of state. For purposes of protocol, the Chairman of the Presidium is usually treated like a "head of state," and therefore the Chairman is frequently referred to as "president" of the Soviet Union. (As with many European parliamentary systems, the title "president" designates the head of state, and is largely for purposes of protocol; the head of the government is the "prime minister." See Figure 2.)

Leonid Brezhnev was the first general secretary of the party to become Chairman of the Presidium of the Supreme Soviet (president). Indeed, he was president twice: from 1960 to 1964, when he helped overthrow Khrushchev, and again from 1977, when he forced Nikolai Podgorny to resign, until his death in 1982. Because both Andropov and Chernenko also assumed the presidency, many observers were surprised when Gorbachev announced that Andrei Gromyko would leave his post as foreign minister to become president as well as a full member of the Politburo. Some said that this amounted to "kicking Gromyko upstairs" so that he could not interfere with Gorbachev's foreign policy initiatives under his own choice for foreign minister, Shevardnadze. Putting Gromyko in the Politburo, however, would guarantee a continuing influence for him, so that the loss of his old ministerial position must not have been too serious a blow.

Like the parliamentary systems of Western Europe, the Soviet government cabinet, or Council of Ministers, is legally responsible to the Parliament (here the Supreme Soviet). (This is

Figure 2 Structure of the Soviet State

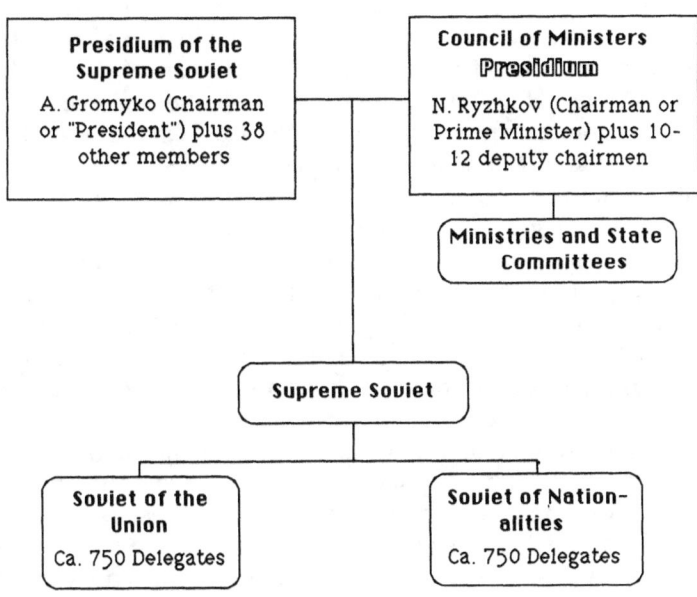

a mere paper responsibility, however, because the members of the Council of Ministers are really dependent on the party leadership, of which they are also a part.) The large number of ministers and agency heads (more than a hundred) that make up the Council of Ministers precludes this body from meeting routinely, so a kind of executive committee, the Presidium of the Council of Ministers (not to be confused with the Presidium of the Supreme Soviet), has been formed. This smaller body is more comparable to Western cabinets, and the chairman of the Presidium of the Council of Ministers is frequently called the Soviet "prime minister." While Stalin and Khrushchev served both as chairman of the Council of Ministers (that is, as "prime minister") and general secretary of the party, thus occupying the top posts in both government and party, there seems to be an agreement since 1964 when Brezhnev became general secretary and Kosygin became prime minister that these positions should be held by different people. Thus, just as General Secretary Gorbachev decided not to follow Brezhnev, Andropov, and Chernenko as "president," he has so far made no attempt to emulate Stalin and Khrushchev and appoint himself prime minister (chairman of the Council of Ministers). However, in September 1985 he replaced Brezhnev's appointee, the octogenarian Nikolai Tikhonov, with Nikolai Ryzhkov. (Tikhonov had replaced Kosygin, the first and only prime minister in Soviet history to retire voluntarily, in this case for legitimate reasons of health.)[5]

Many descriptions of the Soviet system note that the Politburo (party) makes general policy, while the Council of Ministers (state) carries it out. (The Presidium of the Supreme Soviet also makes policy by issuing decrees, but these are in conformity with the directives of the Politburo.) This characterization is generally correct, especially with respect to major issues. On the other hand, state bureaucrats may influence and shape, if not actually determine, policy outcomes, for the huge bureaucracy under the direction of the Council of Ministers is responsible for virtually all aspects of Soviet life, and government experts often possess knowledge and technical skills not common among fulltime party elites. Potential conflict between party and state elites is kept to a minimum by the overlap between party and state positions (e.g., such key state officials as the prime minister, Ryzhkov, and the president, Gromyko, are full members of the party Politburo) and also by the watchful eyes of the party bureaucrats under the Secretariat of the Central Committee, which supervises the state bureaucracy along functional departmental lines.

GORBACHEV AND THE USSR: A NEW ERA OR MORE OF THE SAME?

By mid-1986 only a few members of the party's Politburo and Secretariat were holdovers from the Brezhnev era. Numerous key personnel in the state apparatus had also been replaced. Moreover, most of the new appointees were of a new political generation. But in contrast to the relatively relaxed administration of Brezhnev,[6] and the more or less honorable retirement of numerous officials under Andropov and Chernenko, Gorbachev has ousted large numbers of party and state officials on the grounds of "corruption," "irresponsibility," or "incompetence."[7] In the area of foreign policy, too, Gorbachev has taken a number of initiatives, including a state visit to France in September 1985. He met with President Reagan at the Geneva summit meeting of November 1985, where he expressed an interest in continuing a dialogue with the United States. He has made a number of proposals concerning arms control, some of which appear to represent considerable movement in Soviet positions. (Some of his most dramatic proposals were made at the October 1986 summit meeting in Reykjavik, Iceland.)

Above all he has made it clear that he wants improvement in the ailing Soviet economy. One important element in this goal is his vigorous campaign against alcoholism. He has also identified himself with more positive attitudes toward work and the quality of goods and services produced. He is highly supportive of modern technology and its application in Soviet society. At the same time he has insisted on a more realistic assessment of future economic progress, as demonstrated in the new party program, the first draft of which appeared in the fall of 1985, eight months after Gorbachev assumed power. This was the first revision of a party program since 1961, when Khrushchev promised that the Soviet Union would overtake the West in economic development by 1980. The new program pledges to continue the course toward communism as outlined in 1961, but it rejects the old methods and exaggerated assessments made under Khrushchev and Brezhnev. It also implies the unwillingness of Gorbachev and his colleagues to adopt Hungarian- or Chinese-style reforms.[8]

The focus on the weak economy has been a major characteristic of Gorbachev's first year in office. In terms of impact on Soviet ideology, some observers have even compared Gorbachev's remarks about the Soviet economy to Khrushchev's 1956 speech about political matters at the 20th Party Congress.[9] But this does not mean any rejection or even serious questioning of "the system." Rather, as Bialer and Afferica suggest, Gorbachev and his newly appointed colleagues "attribute their predicament to the failure of leadership":

There is no evidence whatsoever that the new leadership's attitude toward the classical, that is, Stalinist, economic system and the post-Stalin political system contains criticism of its basic foundations. Indeed, Gorbachev and his lieutenants are quite optimistic that the economic system can in fact be made to work well and that the political system is basically sound. Their central proposition is, of course, that what the system needs is better leadership and more effective policies.[10]

The first year of new Soviet leadership under Gorbachev is the theme of this book. It is not yet clear what foundations for change this first year has brought. Some students of Soviet politics assert that "change is in the air,"[11] contending that Gorbachev is an opponent of both the neo-Stalinist hardliner and Brezhnev "do-nothing" camps.[12] Others warn that Gorbachev is not really a reformer at all, in the sense of supporting dramatic change, and that in any case there are serious constraints placed on any reform efforts beyond personnel replacements in the party and state bureaucracies, the military, and other social forces. Whether and to what extent Gorbachev can or even wishes to bring about change in Soviet foreign and domestic policies, and what the nature of this change may be, are important themes in the essays that follow.

NOTES

1. Archie Brown, "Gorbachev: New man in the Kremlin," *Problems of Communism* 34 (May–June 1985), p. 3.
2. See Leonard Shapiro, *The Communist Party of the Soviet Union* (2nd ed.; New York: Vintage Books, 1971), pp. 558–78.
3. Frederick C. Barghoorn and Thomas F. Remington, *Politics in the USSR* (3rd ed.; Boston: Little, Brown and Company, 1986), p. 472.
4. Gary Thatcher, "Gorbachev strengthens hand for economic battle ahead," *Christian Science Monitor* (March 7, 1986), pp. 1 and 32; and *New York Times* (March 7, 1986), p. A3.
5. In December 1986 Gorbachev removed the Kazakh Republic party

leader, Dinmukhamed Kunayev, from the Politburo and replaced him with an ethnic Russian, Gennadi Kolbin. A few days later anti-Soviet rioting by nationalistic elements broke out in the Central Asian Kazakh capital city of Alma-Ata. Reports of the disturbance in the Soviet press represented a sharp departure from the traditional Soviet practice of press censorship or silence regarding such events. See *The New York Times*, December 17, 1986, p. A13 and December 19, p. A1.

6. George W. Breslauer, "The nature of Soviet politics and the Gorbachev leadership," in *The Gorbachev Era*, edited by Alexander Dallin and Condoleezza Rice (*The Portable Stanford*, Stanford, CA: Stanford Alumni Association, 1986), p. 17.

7. Seweryn Bialer and Joan Afferica, "The genesis of Gorbachev's world," *Foreign Affairs* 64, No. 3 (February 1986), pp. 613–14.

8. Gary Lee, "Party program revisions demonstrate Gorbachev's power," *Washington Post* (October 28, 1985), p. A17.

9. Bialer and Afferica, "Gorbachev's world," p. 605.

10. "Gorbachev's world," pp. 609, 611.

11. Alexander Dallin, "The legacy of the past," in *The Gorbachev Era*, op. cit., p. 9.

12. Sidney I. Ploss, "A new Soviet era?" *Foreign Policy* 62 (Spring 1986), pp. 46–60.

2 Gorbachev's First Year: An Overview

Helmut Sonnenfeldt

The chapter by Helmut Sonnenfeldt is based on his keynote address at the University of Richmond symposium. In it he surveys Gorbachev's rapid rise to the top of the Soviet political hierarchy, discusses the new leader's "style," and speculates on his political agenda. In general terms he outlines some of the principal problems facing the new general secretary: inertia at all levels of leadership, a weak economy, and a host of foreign challenges. He advises "strength and flexibility" in the American approach to Gorbachev's foreign policy initiatives, in particular his arms control proposals.

Writing before the 27th Party Congress, Sonnenfeldt speculates as to the Congress's potential significance. Noting that this congress was scheduled to begin on the anniversary of the 20th Party Congress in 1956 at which Nikita Khrushchev gave his famous de-Stalinization speech, Sonnenfeldt observes how most congresses have marked certain milestones in the history of the Soviet Union and the CPSU.

That a conference should be devoted to Mikhail Gorbachev's first year in power is a mark of the expectations associated with his ascent to the top position in the Soviet Union. Early in the tenure of this new Soviet leader unusual efforts have been made to take stock of his programs, fathom what changes may be in the offing, and contemplate on how we are to deal with them.

Mr. Gorbachev is no longer the general secretary of the Soviet communist party with the shortest term of service. He has already outlasted his immediate predecessors. In this regard, it is useful to remember that there have been only seven "supreme" leaders in the Soviet Union since Lenin first assumed power during the Bolshevik Revolution.

Gorbachev is the youngest man to assume the top Soviet leadership position since Stalin did so when he was still in his forties. We have the notion in this country that Gorbachev is very young, but actually he is not that much younger than Khrushchev was in the 1950s when he assumed power, or than Brezhnev was when he took over through a coup that removed Khrushchev in 1964. Both Khrushchev and Brezhnev were in their fifties, only two or three years older than Gorbachev is at present. Yet we have become so accustomed to the aging leadership in the Soviet Union that Gorbachev looks like a big break with the past. Since he has become general secretary, the most rapid changes have taken place in the top Soviet leadership and down the line through the party and government machinery since the Stalinist purges in 1930s. Actually changes began to take place right after Brezhnev died in 1982 and Yuri Andropov became general secretary. They then slackened off after Andropov's death when Brezhnev's close associate Konstantin Chernenko assumed power, but they resumed almost immediately after Gorbachev became the top man.

Lest we get carried away with the notion of a "youth movement" in the Soviet Union, it is worth bearing in mind that the average age of the new people at the top is still somewhat greater than that of those who assumed leadership positions under Brezhnev in the mid-1960s, when the removal of Khrushchev's closest associates was arranged.

In my view, and that of many other observers, Gorbachev has been extremely skillful in accumulating authority and status. Since his political career began in the 1950s, his rise has been remarkably steady and rapid. In approximately thirty years, he has risen from elementary party work and work in the communist youth organizations to the very top of the party, with some important posts in between—a highly unusual career progression. He had powerful patrons—for reasons that are not wholly clear, although it is known that Soviet leaders do keep their eyes out for promising people—and Gorbachev obviously kept his eyes out for promising patrons. Of course, a lot of luck was involved, too.

Some of the most powerful Soviet leaders of the post-Stalinist age came from the same area in which Gorbachev grew up and where he later worked his way up the Komsomol (party youth group) and communist party ladders. It is well known that in the Soviet Union the associations one makes in one's hometown, home district, or in any specific place carry on through much of one's later career. And so it was with Gorbachev. Sometimes, of course, it works against a person when, for example, the top figure in the local or regional group experiences failure—his associates tend to suffer. But in Gorbachev's case it certainly worked to his advantage to have a line to the very top leadership group in Moscow through Mikhail Suslov and later through another leader (Fedor Kulakov) who had also served in the district where Gorbachev was functioning. It is widely reported and believed that because Stavropol, the area in which Gorbachev became party boss, is located in the south of Russia near the Caucasus and serves as a vacation area, he had an opportunity to become acquainted with many of the top Soviet leaders who came there to vacation or take health cures—among them Yuri Andropov, his later close associate and the future head of the Soviet secret police. Leaders who came into contact with Gorbachev evidently considered him able, vigorous, and worth watching and promoting; in turn he obviously did what he could to justify their impression of him and their faith in him.

Eventually Gorbachev made his way to Moscow, where he moved quickly up the political ladder. Brezhnev must have thought highly of him or Gorbachev's advancement in the capital as a secretary responsible for agriculture in the Secretariat of the Central Committee could not have been as rapid as it was. Gorbachev leaped forward into other major positions of responsibility, influence, and power in the Andropov era—all of which increased as Andropov's own health began to deteriorate rapidly in the course of 1983. Gorbachev evidently had the ambition to succeed Andropov directly, but that particular ambition was not realized when Andropov died. Instead, Chernenko, an older man and close associate of Brezhnev, moved into the top job. He was already quite ill and handicapped. As Chernenko's end approached, Gorbachev moved skillfully and purposefully to assure himself of the succession. From all accounts he was not unchallenged, but it is clear that he put together sufficient support to be able to step into Chernenko's shoes almost immediately upon his death. Indeed, the arrangements might have been completed even before Chernenko died, because Gorbachev was appointed general secretary of the Communist party before his predecessor's funeral. This meant that the new general secretary's picture appeared on the front pages of the Soviet press while the obituaries for the late general secretary were relegated to an inside page. This unprecedented achievement was the beginning of Gorbachev's very skillful management, obviously with the support of others, of his own rise to eminence and status.

By coincidence or good fortune, the next Soviet party congress was due to occur within approximately a year of the period when Chernenko became incapacitated and died. Chernenko had desired to have his name associated with a party congress, and plans were made accordingly to move the date of the Congress forward so that he might attend. As it turned out, he died before the congress took place, and the congress fell naturally into the first year of Gorbachev's rule.

One can argue about the significance of party congresses in the Soviet Union. Some think their importance is exaggerated and regard them as preprogrammed affairs, stage-managed by the leadership. Others attribute much more significance to them. As I look back over the party congresses, I am impressed by how virtually all of them, in retrospect if not at the time they were held, marked certain milestones in the development of the Soviet Union and in the evolution of the Soviet Communist Party. Indeed, these congresses, though largely stage-managed and carefully prepared to avoid surprises, do on occasion even develop a dynamic of their own. This occurred in 1956 and on other occasions as well. Thus, while important as symbolic events, they are also occasions for proclaiming and confirming lines of policy as well as for implementing major personnel changes. As such, they sometimes have been events of high drama. It has intrigued me that the date Gorbachev set for the opening of the new Party Congress, 25 February, marks the thirtieth anniversary to the day of Khrushchev's famous "secret speech" at the 20th Party Congress, in which he severely criticized the Stalinist period and Stalin's own behavior. It is almost an aphorism in the Soviet Union that when something unusual happens, it is rarely coincidental, and it strikes me that by selecting the 25th, rather than the 24th or 26th, Gorbachev might have wanted to make some sort of a statement.

In any event, the Congress has fallen within Gorbachev's first year in power, and from Gorbachev's standpoint this is very desirable, as it has accelerated the process of personnel change. Likewise, it has accelerated the process of drafting certain documents traditionally adopted at party congresses and, therefore, gives Gorbachev a formal platform on which to stand, if he so wishes.

Of course, the Party Congress is only one of many events associated with Gorbachev's first year in power. The Geneva summit meeting with President Reagan, his trip to France, and many other events, symbolic or otherwise, have provided him with a means for establishing and conveying his status as the supreme Soviet leader. Though he chose not to assume the formal presidency of the Soviet state (or, perhaps, was not permitted to do so), as his recent predecessors had done, there is no question that he is regarded in the Soviet Union as the top figure in the state and Communist party hierarchies. That does not imply that he may not have some detractors or encounter problems in working his will. But in terms of standing out from the rest and being regarded as the national and international spokesman of the Soviet Union, he has achieved his supreme position in remarkably short order and, I would say, in brilliant fashion. Certainly by Soviet standards, he has been very successful.

Because of his relative youth, many Western analysts routinely refer to Gorbachev as the Soviet leader who will take his country into the twenty-first century and will probably still be in power when perhaps two more U.S. presidents have come and gone. There is almost a monarchical quality to Soviet leadership arrangements, though since the Revolution the "throne" has not passed to blood relatives of the incumbent. Soviet leadership change occurs when age takes its toll or when coups remove leaders by force or at least by strong persuasion. Since Brezhnev's assumption of power, the leaders have grown old in the job and change did not occur until they died. (Before that, Lenin and Stalin also ruled until they died.) This, generally speaking, is also what happens in monarchies. So while Americans wrestle with the possibility of a single six-year term for their president, the Soviets look forward to what may be a fifteen or twenty-five year term for their new leader. In the West many people seem almost relieved to have a seemingly long-term leader once again in power in the Soviet Union. Many prefer political stability to frequent changes with unknown (or relatively unknown) leaders coming to the fore.

It is quite obvious, and routinely commented on, that since assuming power, and to some extent even before, Gorbachev has altered the leadership "style" of the old men who ruled the Soviet Union in recent years. We tend to forget, however, that when they were younger, those old men were also quite vigorous, and that in their prime Khrushchev and Brezhnev, especially Khrushchev, became TV personalities in the West, even in the early years of television. It was often said of both Khrushchev and Brezhnev that had they been born here they might have been elected, if not president, then perhaps mayor of Boston or some similar position. We have not heard such talk about Mr. Gorbachev. Some who have seen him operate at close quarters refer to him as perhaps a "godfather" type. Maybe that is because he lacks the joviality of Khrushchev and Brezhnev, or their sometimes overt brutality. In any case, he is vigorous by any standard. Gorbachev is articulate, as we have seen on our television sets, and as many people have recorded from their meetings with him. In fact, he is something of a compulsive talker once he gets in front of a television camera. He has been highly visible, certainly compared to his immediate predecessors, and he has even engaged in that very rare form of discourse in the Soviet Union—extemporaneous speech. In his first year as general secretary he has visited factories and gone into the countryside "to show himself" to people in various places around the Soviet Union. His occasional off-the-cuff comments have been corrected or modified by the Soviet press, but he has nevertheless felt sufficiently strong and self-assured to speak on live television with various groups of people, and he does it, from all appearances, very effectively. Of course, Gorbachev's visibility is not that of Western leaders who present themselves constantly to the public in parliaments, at press conferences, and so on, but it is quite considerable by Soviet standards. His efforts to influence the outside world, particularly the West, through television interviews and appearances have also made him more visible in the Soviet Union on Soviet television.

In his speeches and remarks he has stressed that he wants to see the bombast removed from Soviet statements and does not want to have himself praised in the fashion of previous Soviet leaders. There is even a report that he threatened to walk out of a meeting of the Supreme Soviet last November, when speakers began praising him in the effusive manner tolerated if not demanded by previous leaders. In direct contact, he is reportedly brisk and to the point; many say he appears well informed about the issues at hand. Yet in press conferences he has not always been as well briefed or informed as he might have been, or he has not always absorbed information as well as he should have. Then again, Gorbachev's speciality has not been foreign affairs, and one should not apply too perfectionist standards. His briskness, directness, and no-nonsense approach led Prime Minister Margaret Thatcher to make her famous remark (during Gorbachev's visit to Britain just before he assumed the top position) that he seemed to be a person one could do business with. Six hours face-to-face with President Reagan at Geneva suggest that he can hold his own in direct discourse, even without doing very much business.

While Soviet strategy for the summit with President Reagan was flawed and tactics were inept, it did show Gorbachev to be quite astute in his assessment of the intangibles of politics. Unlike the sophisticated academician and Americanologist Georgi Arbatov, who at Geneva publicly ridiculed Ronald Reagan's past as a movie actor, Gorbachev not only complimented the president on one of his movies, but also publicly paid tribute to

Ronald Reagan's convictions as a human being, all the while denouncing his policies. Perhaps Gorbachev, better than experts like Arbatov, had absorbed the import of U.S. public opinion polls, which show President Reagan's high personal standing despite criticism of his policies. Incidentally, this distinction between Reagan, the man of conviction, and Reagan, the wrong-headed politician, has continued in the Soviet media. This was not just a spur-of-the-moment remark by the impressionable Mr. Gorbachev after his six hours with Reagan. Rather, he has discovered, like many others, that trashing Reagan personally is not politically a very rewarding activity.

Gorbachev's wife, Raisa, has humanized him in the West and enhanced his media appeal. Although social pages in the Soviet press still do not have quite enough space for general secretaries' wives, pictures including Raisa have occasionally appeared, albeit without captions, even when the event they record was not a funeral. Raisa Gorbachev is not a Krupskaya (Lenin's wife, who was a political figure in her own right). Still, somebody in the general secretary's entourage, perhaps the equivalent of a public relations specialist, went to the trouble of getting her doctoral dissertation into the hands of some West European journalists. It was a dissertation that dealt with life on collective farms in the 1960s, focusing on the Stavropol region, where Mikhail and Raisa lived at the time and where Gorbachev was making a name for himself. The thesis employed some rudimentary (at least by our standards) sociological techniques of data gathering from among *kolkhoz* (collective farm) farmers—and a great deal of anecdotal material. Supposedly some of her conclusions and at least implied suggestions on how to make farming more efficient, rewarding, and humane influenced her husband in the formulation of his own agricultural policies and experiments, first when he was the regional party chief as well as later on. In any case, Soviets have thought it worthwhile to let people in the West draw conclusions of this kind, thus endowing Dr. Gorbachev with a certain political weight.

The new "Gorbachev style" and the rapidity of personnel changes in the first year of the Gorbachev era have raised questions as to whether more fundamental changes are in the offing. Even before he became general secretary, Gorbachev himself raised seemingly fundamental questions concerning Soviet life, society, and politics. Of course, he was not the first Soviet leader to utter criticism of economic and other shortcomings in the Soviet Union. But the very energy and manner with which he has done so imply change. Indeed, he has called for change, sometimes in quite dramatic terms, despite his strictures against using bombastic language. He appears to be suggesting that when he himself uses it, he means it.

Gorbachev has said explicitly that the domestic goals of the Soviet Union, especially those connected with revitalizing and modernizing the sluggish Soviet economy, require peace and good relations with the outside world. He has followed his patron Andropov in reviving Lenin's dictum to the effect that socialism influences world developments most of all by its socioeconomic policies and achievements. Though the notion of the Soviet Union as a model has never been discarded, it has hardly been valid in recent years. "Socialism in one country" turned out to be more accurate as a prediction when Stalin uttered it in the 1920s than as a guide to policy. There has been little in the Soviet experience that anyone would voluntarily wish to emulate. But now Gorbachev seems to be thinking again in older terms of the Soviet Union having its greatest influence on the world through its example. How far he will get with that is, of course, one of the major unanswered questions at this particular stage of his political life.

Many in the Soviet Union clearly expect change, but are not sure what kind to expect. Many advocate change, including a number of people inside the Soviet power structure. But the open question is whether in the end there will be a willingness to adjust the system and change its practices sufficient to the task of transforming and modernizing the economy. Perhaps the most dramatic and revolutionary change to date has been restricting the consumption of alcohol, especially vodka. This is not a trivial measure in the Soviet Union, not just because drunkenness has been a severe problem and has affected health, performance in the work place, and many other aspects of life, but because access to alcohol has been a part of Russian and Soviet life. Perhaps one of the unexpected effects of this series of measures, part of the new general emphasis on discipline, may be that Russians will find in themselves some of the same impulses and incentives for ingenuity to circumvent the rules that Americans discovered during Prohibition. But it would appear that there is a good deal of elite support for rigorous controls on the use of alcohol. Whether those who utter their support sneak a drink now and then is an interesting question, but among members of the Soviet elite concerned with the status and progress of their country, there is a consciousness that alcohol has done much damage to them, and they seem to applaud the measures taken by the new leadership.

The long-term impact of the personnel changes referred to previously is still unclear. What is clear, however, is that they reach deeply and widely into the government and also the party structure. In many cases deputies have been waiting years to move up the ladder. There certainly has been restlessness in the Soviet power structure, but whether this has to do chiefly with impatient people wishing to get their hands on the levers of power or with pressures for genuine change is problematical. In the Soviet system there are, of course, no outsiders in the Western sense, particularly in the U.S. sense, who can be co-opted and brought into the system to rejuvenate it, fertilize it, or shake it up. We know that the co-opting of outsiders in the United States frequently results in large turnover rates that can have very disruptive effects. On the other hand, we do have major pools of creative and energetic people who can be brought into government for periods of time or to make new careers. This simply does not happen in the Soviet Union, where they draw on people already inside the system. There are some who are "less inside" than others, particularly those in some of the academic institutes and similar organizations, where a certain amount of intellectual initiative is encouraged, or if not expressly encouraged, at least taken. Some of these "marginal" insiders, especially those in economic institutes, have been chafing for years under the rigors and rigidities of their system and have advocated reforms and changes based on the experiences of other countries in the Soviet bloc, and most recently, even those of China. It will be interesting to see whether some of these people will enter more directly into the power structure or whether any of their reformist ideas manage to penetrate the center.

Can the top level of leadership overcome the inertia long characteristic of the party ranks, assuming, of course, that it actually wants significant change? Gorbachev and others who have spoken out at the top seem to favor a vigorous center, but one with reduced functions—namely, setting direction and policy rather than engaging in micro-management. They seem to advocate a greater scope for initiative in the system's lower echelons, including at the enterprise level, thereby reducing the role of the bureaucracies and bureaucrats in between. In fact, change of this sort has manifested itself in some measures currently being taken, but a system traditionally based on a strong center and strong centralist orthodoxy may have trouble functioning, even if there is less bureaucracy in the middle, by allowing lower levels to have the sort of initiative and scope of operation that Gorbachev himself professes to advocate. Maybe this tension between authority at the center and enterprise and initiative at lower levels will be resolved by the magic of the dialectic, which we in the West do not enjoy as much as do the Soviets.

Under Gorbachev the economic system seems to be moving in the direction of intensive rather than extensive development. That is, the Soviets hope to achieve growth and dynamism in the economy not by constantly building new plants and expanding the existing base, but rather by increasing productivity in what already exists through greater discipline and injection of modern technology. Of course, there are serious questions as to where the resources to fulfill this policy will be found.

When one considers Soviet approaches to the external regions of immediate concern to the Soviet Union, namely the Soviet bloc in Eastern Europe, one is confronted by a similar problem of potential, or more likely, a real, internal contradiction. Here too the Soviets seem to be advocating more discipline throughout the bloc, more coordination of economic plans and political strategies. Yet at the same time they seem to be offering greater scope for individual countries to satisfy their own national needs and maintain their own national identity.

Can this work in a system like the Soviets', with its traditionally strong center and a strong centrally proclaimed, centrally ordained orthodoxy? From what he has said so far vis-à-vis Eastern Europe, it would appear that Gorbachev does not see the "empire" all that differently from his predecessors. It remains essentially an empire, though the Soviets permit a little latitude now and then on certain issues. The major emphasis, however, has been on discipline and coordination.

In his general foreign policy, Gorbachev has been more active. There have been many Soviet overtures in various directions—toward Western Europe, Japan, China, parts of the Third World, and the United States. Some have argued that a hallmark of his foreign policy is a view of the world that is multipolar rather than bipolar, a world in which there are important players other than the Soviet Union and the United States. This viewpoint supposedly distinguishes him from his predecessors, including former foreign minister, now Soviet president, Andrei Gromyko, who for many years was dominant in the formulation of Soviet foreign policy. But the theory regarding Gromyko's alleged fixation on Soviet–U.S. relations is overdone. The Soviet Union has not been passive in years past with regard to other parts of the world. To be sure, there has not been much imagination or creativity in Soviet policy. It is also true that Gromyko apparently had an utter distaste for going to places like China and Japan and having to listen to old demands and grievances that he had heard many times before—for example, the Japanese territorial issue concerning the Kurile Islands, which the Soviets acquired after World War II. But one cannot paint an accurate picture of the Soviet Union as being totally obsessed with only the United States, or argue that whatever the USSR has done in the Middle East or elsewhere was designed totally and exclusively with an eye toward its impact on relations with the United States. Soviet diplomats and emissaries have recently been flying in and out of Moscow in record numbers; they have been travelling to many different parts of the world. There has been a new assertion of Soviet vigor in several areas in the Third World where the Soviets were already present, such as Angola, parts of the Middle East, Nicaragua, and most recently, South Yemen.

But in terms of innovation or changing approaches, the Soviets have so far been extremely cautious. Whether this is caution "by nature," or Gorbachev's reliance on style over substance to achieve a certain momentum in Soviet policy, is open to question. Despite his political successes at home, Gorbachev still does not have the sort of consensus that would enable him to undertake substantial changes in policy, assuming he wanted to. Soviet initiatives as a whole toward China, Japan, the Middle East, and even the United States have remained cautious and within a very narrow spectrum of conduct. The flood of arms control proposals from Moscow should not be mistaken for readiness to sit down for serious negotiation.

A special sore point in Soviet–U.S. relations has been President Reagan's Strategic Defense Initiative (SDI). It seems to be as much a psychological as a practical military problem for the Soviets, as they see in SDI a U.S. effort to exploit the United States technological and industrial power in order to attain what the Soviets believe Washington thinks will be a substantial military advantage. On the one hand, they claim that SDI cannot possibly work, or, if it does, could easily be defeated by their countermeasures. On the other hand, they seem genuinely to fear that down the road SDI might have a substantial impact on their own military posture and require them to make additional exertions they would prefer not to make at the moment.

Much of their recent diplomatic activity has, in fact, centered on SDI and has constituted an effort to pressure or induce President Reagan, through the prospect of a grand disarmament agreement, to curtail, or indeed to halt, SDI altogether. This was one reason, in addition to his personal desire to enhance his own power, reputation, and stature, that Gorbachev went to the Geneva summit in November 1985. All the signs pointed to an attempt by the Soviets to turn the heat on—to confront President Reagan with the prospect of an unsuccessful meeting unless he gave way on SDI. That strategy obviously failed; Reagan did not yield anything on that issue, despite hours of meetings with Gorbachev and Soviet foot-dragging concerning a final statement. That final statement, while not the grandest possible, was a document of considerable substance. The progress in ameliorating and improving Soviet–U.S.

relations was modest, but one could not have reasonably expected more. Sitting hour after hour with the U.S. president and appearing jointly in front of television cameras added to Gorbachev's stature, and the summit demonstrated Ronald Reagan's mastery of his own particular style. (At the summit in Reykjavik in October 1986, Reagan again refused to yield on SDI, but this time apparently without much mastery of style—editors' note.)

Many people would like to believe that the Soviets will seek to achieve savings in their military programs through deals with the United States, or that Soviet economic realities are such that Moscow may be compelled to seek deals with Washington. There are those who similarly argue that U.S. economic problems, especially the budget squeeze, are such that the United States may be compelled to seek relief through negotiations and agreement with the Soviet Union. It should be noted, however, that the history of previous arms control agreements with the Soviet Union would indicate that major economic savings would probably not result.

If new agreements are to be made, they will have to be much more substantial than anything achieved so far. What was achieved previously, especially in the 1970s, was in fact very modest, despite the major negotiating tasks involved. Now we have serious questions as to whether even those modest agreements are being complied with faithfully and properly.

If Soviet economic problems and the recasting of investment priorities require Soviet leaders to look to their military programs for resources, there are undoubtedly ways in which they can do this on their own without getting involved in complicated negotiations with the United States. Many Soviet programs could be pared down, stretched out, or even forgone. The concentration of Soviet forces opposite China, for example, serves no particular military purpose since there is no threat of a Chinese invasion of the Soviet Union. To maintain these troops at the end of long lines of communications is an expensive proposition. Some published CIA estimates cited in congressional testimony suggest that a certain leveling off in the growth of the Soviet defense budget has already occurred in recent years. There are always disputes about this because of the secretiveness of the Soviet system and the difficulty of getting at the facts. But I believe that if he wished to act and had the requisite support at home, Gorbachev could realize some substantial savings without engaging in major agreements with Washington. Of course, he may be waiting to see what effect budget cuts have on American programs before seriously assessing how much he might have to compromise in any Soviet–U.S. negotiations.

In any case, progress on arms control between the United States and the Soviet Union requires sustained and detailed negotiations as well as negotiators with authority on both sides. In my view, such negotiations have not yet occurred. Proposals have been made publicly and semi-publicly. Delegations have met in Geneva and are meeting there now. But I do not believe they are actually committed to negotiating—sitting down, exploring, trading and writing treaties; rather, they are exchanging catalogues of positions or wish lists, as it were.

Progress in arms control also requires a surrounding environment in Soviet–U.S. relations marked by restraint in crisis situations, and by a more normal set of bilateral relations so that we do not have situations like that involving Professor McClellan at the University of Virginia, who had to wait eleven years for his wife and her daughter to join him. That is just one small case of great importance in human terms to the individuals concerned, but it is also symptomatic of the need for a broader basis of relations if there is to be sustained and serious progress in the area of arms control.

In conclusion, then, there is no clear-cut answer to the question whether there has been any real change or movement in the Soviet Union under Mikhail Gorbachev. What is clear is that Gorbachev, at least for the moment, represents a greater challenge to the United States than his moribund predecessors did. The new general secretary pursues an "activist" style, and he has thrown out lines of communication in several different directions. This activism could, of course, turn into a new Soviet assertiveness, as we have seen to some extent in some of the world crisis areas I mentioned. The new postwar generation may be concerned with demonstrating that the Soviet Union is a vigorous world power—we do not know whether that is uppermost in its mind—or doing something to get the Soviet Union moving again in economic and social terms. Perhaps they think they can do both simultaneously. The direction of Soviet policy toward the United States and the rest of the world is still open to interpretation. That is why we need to maintain a combination of strength and flexibility in our own posture and in our approach to the Soviet Union. We must show that we can and will do business if the other side wants to, but that we have interests that we mean to protect. This is important so that there will be no misunderstanding in some future crisis situation.

3

The Gorbachev Generation
Konstantin Simis

In this chapter on the "Gorbachev generation," Konstantin Simis takes issue with the "optimists" who would believe that Gorbachev's assumption of power signalled the beginning of a wholesale reform of Soviet institutions. He concludes that Gorbachev and his peers are much more interested in preserving that status quo than altering it, and he cautions Western leaders not to be deceived by cosmetic changes. It is his view that although the bottle might have a slightly different shape, the wine remains essentially the same.

Simis pays particular attention to the "new generation" of Soviet leaders, the Gorbachev generation, surveying the backgrounds and qualifications of the cadres who make up Gorbachev's team. Unlike some Sovietologists, he does not believe that the new leaders are technocrats, but rather that "the partocracy sustains itself and blocks the advancement into the ruling elite of psychologically incompatible types, including technocrats."

In his analysis of Gorbachev's "stunning career" in the CPSU, Simis concludes that Gorbachev is much more of a political animal than he is an intellectual, essentially like the friends and associates whose recent promotions he has overseen. His academic training is unimpressive. In the past he has exhibited few "technocratic" or "creative" impulses. Even if he sincerely desired systemic reform, which Simis doubts, he would be opposed by the overwhelming majority of the party leadership who do not desire to rock the boat. In Simis' view, little that Gorbachev has undertaken in his first year would indicate that meaningful reform is around the corner. For him, the partocracy, not a new technocracy, is in the ascendancy, and probably will remain so for a long time to come.

INTRODUCTION

Mikhail Gorbachev's selection as Soviet communist party leader presents the West with many challenges, none more important than figuring out what sort of people will occupy the Kremlin's top positions after this changing of the guard. Dwelling on the characteristics and tastes, or personal biases and inclinations of individual Soviet leaders, is pointless—as the case of Yuri Andropov, whose real and imagined cosmopolitan qualities encouraged some journalists and Sovietologists to predict a sharp upswing in superpower relations, made embarrassingly clear.

Rather, the task is to determine the social psychology of those Soviets age 60 and under who already occupy senior party and government positions—men such as Politburo member Vitaly Vorotnikov, chairman of the Russian Soviet Federated Socialist Republic's council of ministers; his new Politburo colleague Prime Minister Nikolai Ryzhkov; and Politburo candidate Vladimir Dolgikh, Central Committee secretary for industry. What are their value systems and their attitudes toward career problems? What mixture of personal ambition, material desire, ideological commitment, and sense of duty governs their social and political behavior? Sociology in the Soviet Union, which ignores these factors, fails to contribute useful answers. Yet only by constructing such a profile can the West hope to get the data that will make sound predictions about the Gorbachev generation possible.

Some Western Sovietologists already expect this group's social make-up and its foreign and domestic policies to differ significantly from those of the men they have already begun to

"The Gorbachev Generation," by Konstantin Simis, reprinted with permission from *FOREIGN POLICY* 59 (Summer 1985). Copyright 1985 by the Carnegie Endowment for International Peace.

replace—the late party leader Konstantin Chernenko, the late Defense Minister Dmitri Ustinov, former Prime Minister Nikolai Tikhonov and Foreign Minister Andrei Gromyko, the last survivors of the old guard. These analysts believe that the new Soviet generation is dominated by technocrats who will judge policies pragmatically, by the degree to which the country is functioning politically and economically.

If they are right, and the Gorbachev generation's top priority is economic reform, a significant improvement in East-West relations could be expected when this group takes over completely. Logic would dictate that the foreign policy of these pragmatists would strive above all to secure maximum access to Western technology, to obtain Western financial aid, and to increase East-West trade. The ideological myth of Marxism-Leninism—the abolition of capitalism and the worldwide triumph of socialism—would be consigned, to borrow a phrase, to the ash-heap of history.

Unfortunately, the available evidence about the new Soviet generation justifies scant optimism. Gorbachev and his political peers have so far shown every sign that their main interest is preserving the domestic status quo, and especially the political structure through which they have risen. For these leaders are first and foremost creatures of a Soviet system that has evolved into a "partocracy," in which a fusion of the party and government apparatus now permits the former to control completely the legislative, executive, and judicial branches. As a result, Western leaders and analysts should not be fooled by the cosmetic changes and tactical deviations that will be made in Soviet foreign policy in the years to come. Domestically and internationally, what the new generation has in mind is more of the same.

Men no older than their early sixties already hold considerable power in the Soviet ruling elite. Approximately one third of the group comprising full members of the Central Committee of the Communist Party of the Soviet Union (CPSU), members of the Central Committee Secretariat, ministers, and committee chairmen of the Council of Ministers were born in or after 1925. Now, with Gorbachev's elevation to the post of general secretary of the Central Committee, their number will undoubtedly increase. Their careers are hardly a secret to Western specialists. The texts of their public statements are available and the details of their education and training are known. Only in information about their activities in official posts are Western analysts seriously deficient. Thus analysts have some means of determining whether this new generation differs substantively from the old guard, and how these youngsters are going to wield power.

Some Sovietologists who believe that the new political cohort consists of a sociologically distinct group of technocrats are predicting truly epochal changes from the Gorbachev generation. The optimists argue that technocrats will play down ideological rationales and the principles of monopoly and centralization currently favored by the partocracy and, in order to revitalize the economy, will support truly radical change. Gorbachev and his peers will not oppose a genuine curbing of the power of the party apparatus, but will concomitantly encourage the autonomy of the government bureaucracy's direction of the national economy. The Gorbachev generation will not oppose decentralization, they say, and will even introduce elements of a market economy.

The optimists' analysis is based on the fact that all members of this technocratic generation are professionals, have received a specialized education in technical institutes, and will bring to the partocracy their experience in engineering, agronomy, and other professions. Considerable managerial experience in industry and agriculture, and, as a result, firsthand knowledge of the absurdities of centralization, are also attributed to these leaders.

Most members of the new generation do indeed hold advanced degrees. The vast majority acquired on-the-job experience in their fields and supervised factories or industrial associations before becoming secretaries of administrative regions (*oblasts*), Central Committee Secretariat department chiefs, or ministers. Yet so did the old partocrats. All of former Soviet leader Leonid Brezhnev's economic committee chairmen and ministers held degrees in economics, engineering, or agronomy. And all boasted professional or managerial experience. Of 100 leaders who had joined the upper administrative levels of the party and government by the start of 1984, 85 had specialized work experience or held advanced degrees.[1]

As far as current party functionaries are concerned, Soviet sociologists report that all secretaries of party central committees in the Soviet republics and all secretaries of oblast party committees (*obkoms*) have received a higher education. The same sources report that some 75 percent of them are specialists in the national economy and that 99.6 percent of city and district committee secretaries are graduates of technical institutes, with most having work experience in their own specializations and in management.[2] At higher government levels such experience is even more common. In the current Soviet Council of Ministers, all ministers and committee chairmen in charge of industrial, agricultural, and economic ministries and agencies hold advanced degrees; all have professional backgrounds; and all have been executives of major enterprises during their careers.

Yet not one of these officials displays any significant sign of technocratic values. In fact, in its determination to preserve itself and its monopoly of power, the ruling partocracy has created a selective promotion system that makes impossible not only a technocracy's rise to power, but its very formation in the first place. The Soviet system is self-perpetuating. It is governed by a simple but effective principle: promotions to the highest managerial levels, and ultimately to the ruling apparatus, are made not primarily on the basis of any professional training and qualifications or organizational or administrative abilities, but on the basis of loyalty to the partocracy: "ideological maturity" or "loyalty to party interests," as official documents and propaganda call it.

As recently as March 1984, in one of his first speeches as general secretary, Chernenko declared, "The leader of our time must be primarily distinguished by loyalty to the ideas of the party."[3] Such qualifications as organizational ability and professional expertise came in distant seconds. An article in the June 1984 issue of *Voprosy istorii KPSS* (Problems of the History of the CPSU), a journal of the Central Committee, argued that throughout Soviet history the primary criteria for selecting the cadre leadership have been ideological. The partocracy's self-perpetuating selection mechanism has been developed over many years and is nearly foolproof. The Gorbachev generation's social psychology can be identified fairly accurately by examining the system's workings.

A PROCESS OF UNNATURAL SELECTION

First and foremost, the partocracy sustains itself and blocks the advancement into the ruling elite of psychologically incompatible types, including technocrats, by retaining full control of promotions to the managerial level in factories and plants and of all appointments of party or government functionaries. Not a single assignment to an executive post can be filled without party approval.

Rewards and protection are handed out only to those whose loyalty has been tested and proved. The partocratic regime needs loyal, technologically adept servants, but finds dangerous those who might become technocrats. The technocrat by definition favors limiting—or even breaking—the party apparatus' power over the national economy and therefore favors removing from party control those branches of government responsible for industry, agriculture, and finance, including planning bodies. Preventing this mentality from challenging the partocracy is the principal raison d'être for the system created by the Soviet elite, or *nomenklatura*.

The few Soviet sociological inquiries into the structure of the ruling apparatus and the rules governing its formation are rarely made public. One notable exception to this rule was the publication, in 1975 and 1976, of a series of three articles by Aleksandr Levikov in *Literaturnaya Gazeta*.[4] Levikov concluded that promotion in the Soviet Union does not depend on the quality of one's professional work or on personal ability. His evidence: an experiment at a major Leningrad enterprise, where more than one third of workers whom experts had secretly judged to be incapable of supervisory work were nonetheless promoted into executive management positions.

In essence, promotion to executive posts in the Soviet Union is governed by a process of "unnatural selection" in which loyalty is valued over ability and initiative is effectively punished.

In the words of Tatiana Zaslavskaya, an active member of the Academy of Sciences of the USSR:

[Career advancement in general] is oriented not toward activating, but toward repressing, useful economic activity on the part of the population. In exactly the same way initiative of managers of enterprises in organizing production or improving economic contacts is punished or simply nipped in the bud. *Right now the actions of the most "obedient," not the most talented, bold, and energetic, are most often rated most highly, as are those of executive leaders who are not even able to boast of industrial successes* (emphasis added).[5]

As Levikov explains, individuals who have risen through the ranks "are all characterized by 'social activism,'" the system's way of describing the willingness of qualified specialists to abandon their professional activities and dedicate themselves entirely to party, youth group (*komsomol*) or union work—to become professional partocrats. In practice this means that the path from engineer, agronomist, or economist to official, at first within management and then in party or government organs, usually takes aspiring partocrats through a stage of "social"—that is, political—work. This first rung of the partocracy's career ladder gives candidates their first chance to prove their loyalty—usually manifested in their ability to recognize when the partocracy's needs must receive priority over the interests of their enterprises or institutes.

Those who win the trust and sympathy of district party committee functionaries advance to the next stage: what is known as released-time work (*osvobozhdenaya obshchestvennaya rabota*). Much of the party-related work done by CPSU members in social organizations such as unions, komsomols, or party groups is part-time, and something of a mixed blessing. Although chairmen of union committees or secretaries of party bureaus may enjoy all the advantages of these positions, they also must fulfill their professional obligations, and they receive a salary for doing so. Released-time workers, however, form a special group. They are formally relieved of their professional obligations and receive salaries for their work in "social" organizations. Thus they become entry-level, professional functionaries of the partocracy. Sociological studies indicate to Levikov and other Soviet specialists that in 95 cases out of 100, released-time work leads to positions that are stepping stones to ministerial posts and district or regional party secretaryships.[6]

In fact, an analysis of the biographies of 100 functionaries who joined the ruling elite by 1984 reveals the existence of a standard career ladder in Soviet society: professional experience followed by social work, released-time work, promotion to an executive post in the field of specialization, experience in the party or government apparatus, and eventual promotion within the apparatus to a much higher level. Consequently, even before they advance to high-level managerial positions, all professionals ultimately admitted to mid- and high-level positions in the party and government apparatus have proved their aptitude for work in a partocratic system—that is, the obedience and lack of initiative which Zaslavskaya noted.

There is, however, another key ingredient to a successful Soviet political career that Soviet sociologists understandably neglect: the patronage system. Patronage was particularly important during the Brezhnev-Andropov-Chernenko years. Of the 100 functionaries who had moved into the ruling elite by 1984, 66 appear to have been protégés of Central Committee secretaries or Politburo members, including Brezhnev himself.[7] Their unofficial intervention decisively influenced the selection of all 100. The ruling elite's instinct for self-preservation renders remarkably small the possibility of patronage for an individual not sharing the officially prized mentality. This is how the genetic code of the partocracy is reproduced and transmitted; this is how the Soviet system precludes the formation of any group whose particular interests and goals might not coincide with those of the partocracy.

Consequently, not only do few Soviet managers support radical economic reforms that would give them managerial independence from the party apparatus—the ideal of any technocrat—they strongly oppose any such reforms. For example, Zaslavskaya notes in her previously cited essay that high-level managers "are afraid of paying the price for a significant expansion of their rights and income: a sharp increase in their obligations, the growth of stress at work, [and] increased economic responsibility for the results of that expansion." This is the result, she adds, of a "system of industrial relations which, over decades, has chiefly produced a passive type of worker."

Soviet managers are most accurately seen as devoid of the typical technocratic mentality. Psychologically or organizationally, they consider themselves integral parts of the party/government apparatus. Reaching the top of the Soviet career ladder generally takes about 25 years.[8] That is more than enough time for specialists or professional managers to lose, consciously, whatever technocratic traits they may originally have had.

Gorbachev and his most successful peers—Vorotnikov, Ryzhkov, and Dolgikh—fit this description perfectly. Each of these men has followed precisely the career steps outlined above. And their attitudes toward the possibilities of radical economic reform and establishment of a real separation of power and function between party and government apparatuses reveal scarcely any traces of technocratic values.

A radical reform of the Soviet economy cannot take place without eliminating certain organic defects—chiefly, overcentralization and the negligible role played by market forces and by considerations of economic, as opposed to administrative, efficiency. Such reforms, however, would directly threaten the ruling establishment, since they would inevitably lead to limiting its power. Thus any national leaders determined to champion radical reform would pit themselves against all levels of the partocracy, especially their own—the top. Any serious attempt to separate the government apparatus from the party apparatus and to restore some of the government's power and autonomy would soon collide with the same problem—even though the government's power has always been explicitly established by the Soviet constitution.

GETTING AHEAD THE SOVIET WAY

Gorbachev has thus far acquired the most potential for influence on the future development of the Soviet structure. A favorite son of the party apparatus, he has had a stunning career in that hierarchy. Although normally a new party member's climb to full Central Committee membership takes 25 years, Gorbachev made it in 19. Although the average age of new Central Committee members is 49, Gorbachev joined the group at 40. Although new Politburo members average 59 years of age, Gorbachev won this exalted status 10 years earlier in life.[9]

From the beginning of his career, the new general secretary showed a conscious and single-minded resolve to become a professional party functionary. While still a law student at Moscow State University he became secretary of the law school komsomol unit. When he graduated from law school in 1955, before gaining any experience as an attorney, Gorbachev moved directly to the post of first secretary of the City Komsomol Committee in Stavropol.

Thereafter his career proceeded without interruption, gathering speed and remaining exclusively within komsomol and, later, provincial party executive offices. In 1958 he became second secretary of the Stavropol Regional Komsomol Committee; in 1961, first secretary of that body; in 1963, chairman of the office supervising party organs of the Stavropol Party Regional Committee; in 1966, first secretary of the Stavropol City Committee of the CPSU. Finally, in 1970 he became first secretary of this body, a post that entitled him to election to the Central Committee the following year. Moreover, if the right circumstances converged, the path to the Central Committee Secretariat lay before him. And indeed, only one year later, Gorbachev was elected a full member of the Central Committee. In 1978, at the age of 47, he became a Central Committee secretary and in two years became the Politburo's youngest full member.

Thus Gorbachev matured and developed without a single day's experience either in his profession or in government bodies. Such a career hardly signals a readiness to limit, for the sake of technocratic and managerial ideals, the power of the party apparatus that nurtured him.

The new general secretary's education suggests no such bent, either. Soviet law schools give no more than a general background on theories of state and law, and not much more on the fundamentals of legislation. Nor could Gorbachev have received from his constitutional and comparative law courses a realistic understanding of Soviet or Western political structures and administrative functions. In Soviet universities these classes aim primarily at brainwashing the young. A course in Soviet constitutional law, for example, confines itself to introducing students to the constitution and to the staggering number of scholarly treatises it has generated—despite their almost total irrelevance to Soviet politics and society. And comparative law courses give Soviet students a completely distorted picture of Western democracies.

Students who recognize the falsehoods of official dogma can, through sources of information outside the university, piece together a more accurate view of reality. Gorbachev, however, was apparently not one of these. According to personal conversations I had in Moscow with Lev Yodovich, who was a law school classmate of the new general secretary, from the start Gorbachev was less interested in academic studies than in political activities.

It is true that Gorbachev also received a diploma from the Stavropol Agricultural Institute in 1967. But he received that degree after completing a correspondence course he enrolled in during his term as first secretary of the Stavropol City Committee. He was, in other words, the boss of the directors and faculty of the Stavropol Agricultural Institute; on him depended not only much of their professional success, but also their chances for perks such as decent housing. Thus Gorbachev's degree in advanced agricultural science does not necessarily signify a profound knowledge of agricultural technology or of the organization of Soviet agricultural production, and neither of his degrees stamps him as a technocrat inclined to carry out radical economic reforms or to limit the party's power.

No technocratic impulses emerged during Gorbachev's years as first secretary of the Stavropol Regional Committee, either. He did implement the system of "brigade contracts" endorsed by the Central Committee for this key agricultural region. Unlike the usual brigade system used in Soviet collective farms, the contract system established a direct link between the quality and quantity of goods produced and rewards bestowed—in brief, it incorporated elements of the market economy into Soviet agriculture. Yet Gorbachev's support betrays no penchant for bold innovation. The idea of limited experiments with brigade contracts has long been endorsed by both the Politburo and the Central Committee.

In fact, the only noteworthy original contribution that Gorbachev has made to Soviet agriculture has been the now-discredited Ipatovsky method of harvesting, named after the region in which this experiment was tried. Under this scheme, every district created mobile units for gathering, transporting, and processing harvested foodstuffs. But by placing these units under the control of local political leaders, this scheme significantly curtailed the autonomy of each collective and state farm and poked the party's nose deeper into agriculture. The Ipatovsky method proved grossly ineffective and gradually disappeared. It remains only as evidence of Gorbachev's partocratic mentality and of his attachment to maintaining party control over the economy.

Gorbachev's speeches on economic reform and party/government relations reveal the same leanings. Of particular interest are an address quoted in *Pravda*, March 18, 1984, focusing on problems in the agro-industrial complex, and a speech made at a session of the Supreme Soviet on April 11, 1984, that introduced Chernenko as a candidate for chairman of the Presidium of the Supreme Soviet.

In the first speech, the then-second secretary of the Central Committee had every opportunity to spell out his creed. But only two salient points emerge from the collection of politically acceptable clichés he recited. The first was Gorbachev's support of harvest procedures similar to the brigade contract method. Gorbachev's second point consisted of a call for greater separation between party and government organs in the economic activities of agricultural enterprises. Indeed, he criticized as abnormal situations "when the regional party committees interfere in matters which fall within the direct competency of specialists and economic supervisors."

Yet these apparently technocratic suggestions must be evaluated in context. Actually, the CPSU Central Committee solidly supports the kind of economic-agricultural organization that Gorbachev outlined. Indeed, typical partocrats are among its main proponents. For example, on July 6, 1984, *Pravda* published an article entitled "Developing Contract." Its author was

Nikolai Priezzhaev; far from belonging to the "young" generation in whom supporters of the technocrat theory place their hopes, he is the 65-year-old first secretary of the Ryazan Party *Obkom* and has been a party functionary since 1949. Moreover, in the last two years many party and government leaders—including Chernenko himself, who hardly qualified as a technocrat—have voiced support for some clear delineation of party and government authority. Thus Gorbachev, in his March 18 speech, was simply reiterating a standard Politburo position. A July 5, 1984, *Pravda* editorial put the case more clearly: Citing a speech by Chernenko, it called for just such a demarcation of authority—but emphasized that party organs must, as before, control and direct the activities of government organs and economic organizations.

The bulk of Gorbachev's April 11 speech was devoted to an unprecedentedly explicit attempt to construct a powerful theoretical basis for a political shift opposed staunchly in both Soviet constitutional theory and official propaganda—the merger of the government and party apparatus into one ruling organization that would preserve the latter's supremacy. Breaking with tradition, Gorbachev stated directly that in the Soviet Union "the Party has defined and continues to define the main areas of work of all the components of our political system and, above all, of the Soviet *state*" (emphasis added).

Thus the available evidence labels Gorbachev as a staunch defender of the partocracy. And there do not seem to be any foreseeable external factors that might force him to limit the total authority of this apparatus and, consequently, his own personal power. Further, Gorbachev's three leading contemporaries—Vorotnikov, Dolgikh, and Ryzhkov—all owe their success to similar climbs through the partocracy's ranks. In the 25 or 30 years it has taken them to reach the top, as in their prior managerial positions, they have had ample opportunity to prove their loyalty to their chief patron, the partocracy itself. Therefore, as full-fledged partocrats their behavior as dominant members of the Politburo can be expected to proceed from the premise that what is good for the partocracy is good for them. The same can be said about most of the first secretaries of obkoms.

THE PRICE OF RADICAL REFORMS

History shows, however, that such rigid determinism is not always justified. Political leaders have not always acted in the interests of their social classes. In the mid-nineteenth century, when the salvation of the entire socioeconomic system required dealing a deathblow to the nobility, Tsar Alexander II, "the premier nobleman of Russia," did not flinch from promulgating the most fundamental of economic reforms, the abolition of serfdom.

Closer to the present, nothing in the career of Joseph Stalin's favorite, Nikita Khrushchev, suggested that he would become a reformer. Yet once he had become first secretary of the party's Central Committee and had consolidated his power as chairman of the Council of Ministers, Khrushchev pressed a series of economic and political reforms, including several intended to destabilize the party apparatus and partially limit its power.

Yet Khrushchev, completely uneducated, crude, and ungovernable, was a surviving member of that decimated generation of Bolsheviks that retained much of its revolutionary, ideological fervor. Despite the trauma of Stalinism, these survivors chafed under the post-World War II bureaucratization of Soviet politics and society. Gorbachev, with his two diplomas and his ease in sophisticated society (one cannot imagine him pounding the table with his shoe at the United Nations), belongs to the generation of communist leaders whose first priority is consolidating its personal power.

Nevertheless, Gorbachev may yet understand that only radical reforms can ward off economic disaster and may display sufficient wisdom and leadership to limit the power of the party apparatus in the interests of the country. Nor can one exclude the possibility that Gorbachev will embark on a strategy similar to V.I. Lenin's New Economic Policy (NEP) of 1921. Then, Bolshevism's founder, in a tactical about-face, briefly subordinated Marxist dogma and his own ideals and sympathies to a sweeping program that temporarily injected market practices into Soviet agriculture, small industry, trade, and services. Yet whose fate would await Gorbachev if he did turn out to be a closet reformer—that of Lenin, who successfully carried out the NEP and saved the Soviet regime, or that of Khrushchev, whose experiment led to his own fall from power? Categorical answers should be viewed skeptically. But the system in which Gorbachev and his generation function is different from the one that Lenin knew, and his personal position is different from Lenin's. Until 1921 one could still openly dispute Lenin's proposals and yet retain one's place in the party and government leadership. Lenin's personal authority, however, was so great that no one could seriously challenge his leadership or interfere with his implementation of a particular political line. Moreover, the party apparatus had not yet amassed enough power to challenge Lenin's decision.

If he initiates radical reforms, Gorbachev will be opposed by a powerful, well-organized CPSU apparatus that controls Soviet life on every level. Despite stringent internal party discipline and the complete subordination of lower party levels to upper ranks, the party apparatus today can sandbag reformist plans devised even by the general secretary. Fear of antagonizing too much of this apparatus evidently persuaded Andropov to limit his heralded anticorruption drive to a handful of highly visible targets. When it must, the apparatus can also engineer a palace revolution and oust a leader it deems unacceptable, as in Khrushchev's case. The Politburo conspiracy to oust Khrushchev succeeded so easily precisely because it was fully supported by the party apparatus and by the KGB, whose chairman, Vladimir Semichastny, personally participated in organizing the plot. History suggests that a partocracy that is even stronger today would deal similarly with Gorbachev.

An extraordinarily skillful politician might still overcome these obstacles. But radical reforms would fundamentally alter not only the Soviet economy but also the Soviet political system. The party apparatus would have to lose at least some of its totalitarian character, and major changes in the partocracy would be inevitable as well. Gorbachev has showed no signs of being prepared for political liberalization.

He and his cohorts are likely to handle their country's crises by strengthening the partocracy's power over all areas of life. Some partial reforms in industrial and agricultural planning aimed at minimizing some of the system's worst flaws may be attempted. But even minor reforms will be impossible without some economic liberalization—which would undoubtedly force future Soviet leaders to intensify repression in order to ensure that liberalization did not spread into the social and political spheres.

The new Soviet leaders will have several foreign policy options, ranging from establishing a normal, yet cool, businesslike relationship with the West to deliberately heightening tensions. Their choices will depend not only on domestic and international circumstances but also on the extent to which they can accurately judge those situations.

The available data, unfortunately, suggest that not one of the new leaders—except for the former ambassador to the United States, Anatoly Dobrynin, newly appointed to the Secretariat—has the personal experience or the education to understand how Western democracies function, to measure the sincerity of Western initiatives, or to gauge Western resolve. Indeed, they may believe in the mythical image of the West long purveyed by Soviet propaganda. Understandably, the new Soviet leaders lack the experience of the diplomats and foreign policymakers of the first Soviet generation, many of whom had previously lived in Western countries for many years. Nor do they have the expertise of their contemporaries who graduated from the Foreign Ministry's Institute of International Relations and its Diplomatic Academy and who possess a solid understanding of geopolitics and a fluency in foreign languages that allows them to use Western sources. Individuals with that kind of expertise are by and large restricted to medium-level foreign ministry jobs, diplomatic posts, and Central Committee advisory positions.

Nor has the Gorbachev generation had much personal contact with the West. The Soviet foreign delegations with whom these men have traveled associate as a rule only with Soviet embassy officials, host-country representatives directly relevant to the mission of the visit, and members of carefully selected private groups: communist parties, bilateral friendship associations, and disarmament activists. Such contacts hardly provide a complete picture of Western life. Despite—or perhaps because of—the attendant hoopla, it is unlikely that Gorbachev left England after his December 1984 visit with an accurate impression of British democracy or one of its key pillars, a free press.

Highly qualified advisers can partly compensate for the expertise gap at the top. But their role should not be overrated. In the Soviet system, as in any bureaucracy, consultants, either consciously or unconsciously, tend to give their superiors advice that these superiors want to hear. In the USSR this ubiquitous law operates especially effectively, for the Soviet advisers who irritate their superiors in the Central Committee apparatus, or in its secretariat, run the real risk of losing their jobs and, perhaps more important, a series of perks that not even academic specialists and journalists in the field enjoy: access to Kremlin stores, hospitals, and sanatoriums; chauffeured limousines; and apartments in what are by Soviet standards luxury buildings reserved for the elite.

The Gorbachev generation's partocratic mentality, its ignorance of the West and of foreign affairs in general, and its likely domestic policy of economic liberalization with greater political repression suggest that under this generation, Soviet foreign policy will follow a pattern established during the 1970s: a determination to reap the strategic advantages of political and military pressure on the West, both in Europe and in the Third World, coupled with a drive to gain Western economic resources. This policy should please the military. Continued high international tensions may give the Gorbachev generation not only a valuable pretext for tightening the screw domestically but also a handy excuse for the economic failures and further drop in living standards that token reforms will not be able to prevent. Moreover, all the while, the West can expect a continuing series of peace offensives designed to undermine domestic and NATO support for appropriately firm responses.

In fact, Soviet–U.S. relations could shortly return to a rough approximation of 1970-style détente. The Kremlin's repression of social and political rights and efforts to isolate Soviet citizens more completely from unmonitored contacts with foreign visitors and with the outside world will not necessarily hinder this development. Nor will the presence of a conservative U.S.

president, so long as he avoids public support for the human rights movement in the Soviet Union. After all, détente's zenith came under that ideal representative of the partocracy, Leonid Brezhnev, and a conservative Republican president, Richard Nixon. Together with his exceedingly pragmatic adviser, Henry Kissinger, Nixon dropped the human rights question from the public agenda of U.S.–Soviet relations, despite Moscow's crackdown on human rights activists during the early 1970s.

This period in U.S. foreign policy demonstrated that it is possible for Washington and Moscow to arrive at some beneficial agreements of real significance. Yet détente also showed the dangers of basing America's Soviet policy on wishful thinking. Both lessons should be remembered as the United States formulates its policy toward a Soviet adversary led by the Gorbachev generation.

AFTERWORD

Gorbachev has been in power now for more than a year. During this time he has done much to consolidate his power: he has replaced a significant number of first secretaries of the territorial party committees, namely those who constitute the backbone of the party apparatus and directly govern the population. He has given youth to the Politburo by removing from it his opponents and replacing them with supporters who belong to his own generation. The 27th Party Congress gave Gorbachev the opportunity to change about 40 percent of the party's Central Committee and to install his own supporters. By replacing the chairman of the Council of Ministers as well as a number of other ministers and their assistants, he also has significantly altered the composition of the upper link of the state apparatus.

Thus, during the time Gorbachev has been in power, he has demonstrated an ability to strengthen his position and, to a significant degree, he has brought a group of younger leaders into the party/state apparatus. From these facts we can establish that there is in power a generation of leaders, approximately 60 and younger, who, as several Sovietologists in the

West propose, have been called to carry out radical economic reform including nothing short of rejecting central planning and its management of agricultural and industrial enterprises or of limiting the power of the party apparatus over these enterprises.

To what extent have Gorbachev and the other new Soviet leaders turned these hopes into reality? During the year since the installation of a new general secretary, have any measures been implemented that limit the power of the central planning directorate and the management of the economy or substantially increase the independence of enterprises?

Practically nothing in this area has been accomplished. Much has been said about the necessity of giving managerial and financial independence to the enterprises, while in practice everything remains within the framework of experimentation begun even before Gorbachev. The fact, however, that several enterprises are working under experimental conditions has no effect on the structure of the Soviet economy and does not alter the system of central planning and management. There are promises of broader rights for the enterprises, but as yet nothing has been done to assure their fulfillment. Furthermore, Gorbachev himself, speaking of the necessity to strengthen the managerial and financial independence of the enterprises, consistently underscores the firm resolve of the government to strengthen, at the same time, the time-tried method of centralized management and planning.

Gorbachev says nothing of how to combine these two incompatible tendencies. However, it is perfectly clear that it is not possible to increase the independence of the enterprises from the ministries and from central planning and, at the same time, to strengthen the power of these ministries over the enterprises.

Of course, one year is hardly adequate time to effect change in such an enormous, inert system such as the Soviet economy. Yet we would expect that the new generation of Soviet leaders, led by Gorbachev, plans to reform the system of managing the economy in the coming years. We must consider, however, two documents: "The Program of the Communist Party of the Soviet Union" and "Basic Directions of the Economic and Social

Development of the USSR," which were accepted by the 27th Congress of the Communist Party and which will determine the paths of development in the Soviet Union to the year 2000. In neither of these documents is there anything that testifies to the intention of the ruling authorities to make any kind of substantive changes in either the economic or political structure of the country during the course of the next fifteen years.

To begin with, the stumbling block to effecting radical economic reform is the necessity of limiting the power of the party apparatus over the enterprises. The predicament of the collective farms exemplifies that very dependency of enterprises on the regional and territorial committees of the communist party, which is one of the decisive factors that has brought about the deep crisis in the Soviet economy. Legally, the collective farms enjoy complete financial and managerial independence; but in fact they are completely subordinate to the regional and territorial committees of the communist party. The lamentable results of this dependency are only too well known and do not need to be proven; for example, the absence for the collective farm workers of any material incentive to improve the quality of their work.

Yet it is clear that Gorbachev and his government have no intention of limiting the power of the party apparatus over the national economy. This is stated with sufficient clarity both in "The Program of the CPSU" and in the "Basic Directions of the Economic and Social Development of the USSR." "Basic Directions" contains a statement on the necessity "of a united political and economic leadership. . . . " In official Soviet jargon, this means only one thing: the preservation of the party's leadership in the economy of the country. There is an even more open statement of this in "The Program of the CPSU," in which there is a direct declaration to the effect that all links of the Soviet system function under the leadership of the party.

It is true that at the 27th Party Congress both main speakers—Gorbachev and Ryzhkov, the new Chairman of the Council of Ministers—spoke of the necessity of making reforms in the management of the economy. From the speech by the latter, however, it is clear that by "radical reform" of the methods of management, the party has in mind only the wider adoption in all branches of industry of that program presently in effect for all those enterprises that were included in the experiment already begun before Gorbachev came to power. But it must be understood that although all the enterprises participating in the experiment did, in fact, obtain some degree of independence in the use of financial resources, on the whole, as before, they remain under the direction of the plans and the ministries, and, of course, remain dependent on the party apparatus, that is, on the regional and territorial committees of the CPSU and on the departments of the Central Committee of the Communist Party.

The contents of those sections of "The Program of the CPSU" and "Basic Directions of Development" devoted to the problems of improving the system of managing the economy also indicate that Gorbachev has no intention of weakening the role of central planning or the control of enterprises by the state and party organs. In both of these documents, it is categorically affirmed that the intention of the party is not only *not* to weaken the role of the central planning directorate and management, but, on the contrary, to strengthen it. In "Basic Directions of Development," it is stated directly: the party plans "to strengthen the initiative of centralization in the management of the economy." And "The Program of the CPSU" declares that "the party deems it necessary to heighten the role of planning as an instrument in realizing the economic success of its political program."

In conclusion, the new generation of Soviet leaders, and Gorbachev personally, do not yet have any intention either of bringing about original radical economic reform that would give enterprises managerial independence, or of introducing elements of the free market into the national economy, or of limiting the power of the party apparatus over the economy. In other words, the current leaders of the USSR propose to run the national economy not as technocrats, but as partocrats.

NOTES

1. Alexander G. Rahr (comp.), *A Biographic Directory of 100 Leading Soviet Officials* (Munich: Radio Free Europe/Radio Liberty, 1984).

2. N. Nikolayev, "V. I. Lenin and the CPSU on the selection and advancement of the leading cadres," *Voprosy istorii*, No. 6 (1984).
3. *Pravda*, 7 March 1984.
4. A. Levikov, "Kak stat' ministrom," No. 45 (1975); "Etash cheshkova," No. 51 (1975); and "Professionaly upravleniya," No. 5 (1976).
5. T. Zaslavskaya, "O neobkhodimosti bolee uglublennogo izucheniya v SSSR sotsial'nogo mekhanizma razvitiya ekonomiki," *Forum* (Munich), No. 5 (1983); p. 153.
6. See, for example, M. N. Rutkevich and F. P. Filippov, *Sotsialnye peremeshcheniya* (Moscow, 1970), pp. 105–106.
7. *100 Leading Soviet Officials*, op. cit.
8. Eberhard Schneider, *Die zentrale politische Führungselite der UdSSR*, pt.2 (Cologne: Bundesinstitut für ostwissenschaftliche und internationale Studien, 1982), p. 127.
9. *Ibid.*, 126–129.

4 Soviet Foreign Policy Under Gorbachev: Goals and Expectations
Dimitri K. Simes

Like Konstantin Simis, Dimitri Simes is somewhat at odds with those who see in Mikhail Gorbachev a reform-minded Soviet leader who wants to meet the West half way. In his analysis of Soviet foreign policy under Gorbachev, Simes concludes that the basic goals of this policy remain the same as before, although the means of attaining these goals may be changing. Noting the economic weakness of the Soviet Union, the limited appeal of Soviet culture, and the waning ideological attractiveness of Soviet style communism, Simes concludes that increasingly the Soviets may have to rely on military power as the most appropriate means for securing their various diplomatic and geopolitical ends. On the one hand, Simes finds Gorbachev's recent proposals to eliminate nuclear weapons "a very forthright and creative Soviet concession." On the other hand, he is suspicious of the general secretary's motives, suggesting that a nuclear arms control agreement would enable the USSR to expand and upgrade its conventional forces. For Simes, Gorbachev's "peace initiative" must be considered in light of other recent Soviet foreign policy initiatives in the Middle East, Angola, Libya, and Afghanistan. Simes points out, for example, that under Gorbachev, Muammar Khadafy travelled to Moscow as an honored guest, and 20,000 additional Soviet troops moved into Afghanistan. In conclusion, Simes poses an interesting question: just how much do Gorbachev's Western (especially U.S.) well-wishers really want him to succeed? Many writers discuss Gorbachev's intent to build a healthier economy. But a stronger Soviet economy would probably result in an even stronger Soviet military machine. Is that what the West wants?

The purpose of this chapter is to address Soviet foreign policy—its goals and the expectations of those who formulate it. This is an appropriate subject, because I believe that basic Soviet foreign policy goals under Mikhail Gorbachev remain essentially the same as before; however, foreign policy expectations and the way the Soviets now go about realizing them are very different indeed.

It is general knowledge that the Soviets have been trying for decades to be more like the United States in terms of technological know-how and economic and military strength. Both countries are global powers, have tremendous military arsenals, believe that they have worldwide geopolitical interests, are somewhat messianic in their international outlook, and believe very strongly that they have something unique to offer to mankind. Because of their great size, both are somewhat self-centered. Yet, in spite of these similarities, the Soviet Union and the United States are profoundly different.

It was not Gorbachev or any other Soviet leader, but the Russian tsar, Alexander III (1881-1894), who, according to his foreign minister, observed that the diplomatic service in Russia was becoming too independent; that diplomacy was a deplorable art; that whenever one has to rely on diplomacy, it means that one's foreign policy has failed. The strong accomplish what they need unilaterally, without diplomacy. When one has to make arrangements, when one is forced to compromise, it means that something is fundamentally wrong.[1] When Alexander III died, it was decided to build a monument in his honor. The late tsar's ministers wanted to issue a manifesto describing Alexander as a peacemaker, because he had never engaged in a major war. But the new tsar, Nicholas II, took offense. He said that his father was a great tsar, a warlord, not a peacemaker, and not afraid of anyone. Why did the ministers want to offend him like that?[2]

Another anecdote that reveals differences in the approaches

of the two superpowers is based on an experience I had several years ago in Vienna, Austria, when I had a chance to talk to a leading Soviet political commentator. During our conversation I found that this person was rather offended by the notion that the president of the United States was suggesting that the Soviet Union was interested in war, or that the Soviets would consider war as a policy tool. Reminding us that the Soviet Union had lost twenty million people during World War II, he noted that there was probably not a single family untouched by the war. Russian experiences during the war were completely different from those of the United States, for the whole country had been affected and much of it devastated. If this was the case, we asked, then what were the Soviets doing in Afghanistan? His response was that the action in Afghanistan was not war; it was merely a police operation to help a friendly government. Then he volunteered—our meeting was during the Polish crisis: "If we have to move into Poland, that would be a punitive action." What this commentator was trying to say was that from the Soviet standpoint there is a profound difference between "real war" and a minor intervention, even if one is talking about a rather prolonged action such as the Soviet intervention in Afghanistan. The war which the Soviets do not want, absolutely do not want, is one of major proportions, a nuclear or even a conventional war in which cities are destroyed, millions of innocent people are killed, and the whole country is devastated. Perhaps even more than most Americans, they do not want such a war. On the other hand, using military force as a policy tool and losing 10,000 or 15,000 soldiers as a consequence, as is the case in Afghanistan, is perfectly acceptable to the Soviet leadership—and not particularly objectionable to the Soviet people who recognize that this was the way Russia was built and maintained as an empire.

It is true, of course, that the application of force has been a factor in American history as well. That the Mexicans surrendered Texas; the Spanish, Cuba and the Philippines, and the American Indians, the whole continent was not just the result of peaceful U.S. diplomacy. But I still maintain that there is a fundamental difference between Russian and U.S. approaches to force and diplomacy. Indeed, they are almost incompatible.

Of course, today one must ask about the current Soviet situation, not just the Russian past. To what extent are the Soviets obliged to rely on force as opposed to diplomacy? If one travels around the world, one finds U.S. businessmen almost everywhere. Even in South Yemen, a country that is something between an independent state and a Soviet naval base, there were some U.S. entrepreneurs who managed to get out of the country during the civil war there in January 1986. On the other hand, if one travels around the world, one does not find Soviet businessmen. There are some prestige projects: the Aswan Dam in Egypt, certain major projects in India, and some other huge symbolic enterprises to which the Soviets contributed. But if one is talking about the real economic infrastructure in the Third World, the Soviets are conspicuous by their absence. In many respects economic stagnation in the Soviet Union together with technological progress in the Third World make the Soviets irrelevant and obsolete.

When I went to Damascus for the first time in 1981, I found a Soviet television set in my hotel room. When I was there the last time, it had been replaced with a Syrian-made television, and there was an important difference: it worked. The Soviets are now encountering problems in their trade with India, not because India is moving away diplomatically from the Soviet Union, but because Indian scientists and engineers in many respects are equal if not superior to the Soviets, and they want U.S. know-how and Japanese know-how—that is, Western technology—not what the Soviets have to offer. Due to their economic situation, the Soviets have great difficulty displaying entrepreneurial initiative abroad, since they are unable to do so in their own country. As a result, the Soviets cannot compete economically with the United States or with the West in general.

What about the Soviet ideological appeal? Again, it is increasingly nonexistent. We read about all the spies today—the Walkers and others. What is remarkable is that these are people of very unimpressive caliber. They are people who work for the Soviets primarily out of greed, or in a few cases, because of some unfulfilled personal ambition. One should remember that in the 1930s there were thousands and thousands of people in the West—first class people, intellectuals, politicians, members of the upper classes—who were doing extremely well for themselves and who considered it an honor and a moral duty to spy or do whatever was necessary for the Soviet Union. People like that do not spy for the Soviets anymore. And when one turns to the Third World, in countries like India or even in Africa, one finds increasingly that local elites may be interested in the Soviet system of control, in Soviet methods of remaining in power, but they are not interested in the Soviet political and economic model. It seems clear that the nature of the Soviet ideology has changed to such an extent that it is no longer applicable to any country outside of the Soviet Union.

When the Bolsheviks came to power, many of their leaders could be described as cosmopolitan intellectuals, people who were at home in London, Paris, and Geneva as much as they were in Moscow. Lenin not only spent his formative years in the West, he could write very well in English. He was a leader of the international Socialist movement, and he was genuinely interested and active in the affairs of Swiss and German socialist parties. Somebody like Karl Radek, a member of the Bolshevik Central Committee, was also a member of the German Social Democratic Party. Feliks Dzerzhinsky, founding father of the Cheka (secret police), was very active in the Polish Socialist Party, and one could easily continue the list. But in addition to being cosmopolitan in terms of their personal orientation, these people also represented an international revolutionary ideology. When they came to power in Russia, they thought in a way it was an accident of history. Marx, after all, predicted that the revolution would start in industrialized Western Europe, in England or in Germany. Russia was, in his opinion, far too backward to become the mother of revolution. But as a result of this accident of history, World War I, and the collapse of the Russian Empire, the Bolsheviks saw their chance and they grabbed it. Still, most of them operated on the assumption that unless they could export the revolution, they would not survive. For them, the export of the revolution was not a luxury, it was a basic necessity, because they felt very strongly that sooner or later the capitalist West would unite forces against the young Soviet Republic and destroy it. Accordingly, the export of revolution was nothing short of basic survival. The Bolsheviks who were internationalists were also revolutionaries and, of course, they were great historical optimists. They felt very strongly that history was on their side, that they represented manifest destiny, and that the so-called correlation of forces was constantly changing in their favor.

Now, of course, the Soviets are still officially Marxist-Leninists, but instead of being internationalists, they are increasingly nationalists. Instead of trying to reshape their country and mankind, they are talking, at least in their own sphere of influence, about preserving the status quo. They have just adopted a new party program at the 27th Party Congress. This is going to present them with a unique problem, because for the first time in Soviet history, communism is no longer going to be the practical objective. We still call the Soviet Union a communist country but they appear to be dropping communism as a practical objective. Of course they are keeping it in the program as a kind of beautiful dream which they are going to achieve sometime in the very distant future. But they are saying that they are still in the stage of what they call advanced socialism. They are going to continue building this advanced socialism for decades to come. It is a much more modest expectation than anything they were willing to articulate in the past. In addition to that, for the first time in their history they did not claim at their recent Party Congress that the correlation of forces is changing in their favor. The last time they made this assertion was in 1982, and that was in spite of many setbacks, both at home and abroad. Now, all they are saying is that they can hold their own, that they will not be pushed around, and that they are a superpower second to none. They are not promising that they will succeed in the competition with the United States. That is a very major scaling down of their expectations and that, of course, makes the whole ideology much less appealing to anyone outside of the Soviet Union. The basic point is that theirs is increasingly a nationalist and a conservative ideology.

And what about the appeal of Soviet culture? The Soviets complain constantly that the Americans do not know enough about Soviet culture, and that the Soviet writers who are known in the United States are primarily dissident emigres. While working on an article a few months ago, I read a speech delivered ten years ago by the Secretary General of the Soviet Writer's Union, Georgi Markov, who had a list of complaints about Western disinterest in Soviet authors. What is interesting is that when he listed Soviet writers who he thought were very important but who with two exceptions were unknown in the United States, he included writers who since then have been expelled from the Soviet Union or have emigrated and who now live either in the United States or in Western Europe. Of course, the Soviets still have the Bolshoi ballet and some interesting movie directors, most of whom are now moonlighting in Hollywood, but basically the influence of Soviet official culture is very limited abroad, not only in the United States but also in Western Europe and in the Third World. If one is in Damascus and wants to watch television, one views "Kojak" or "Dynasty." One would not see any Soviet television series, because they just happen to be plainly boring. So, with culture also the Soviets have a problem competing with the West.

One might ask, then, how the Soviets should react when they are lectured by the United States about rules of international competition, when they are told, in effect, "Let's compete, but let's compete peacefully, without relying on force and coercion. Let's compete economically, let's compete politically, let's compete culturally." What do the Soviets hear? They hear, "Let's compete with your hands tied behind your back!"

The Soviets have one tool that works very well for them, although not without some problems: their military machine. One might ask how relevant the Soviets would be in Central America or in Angola, or in the Middle East in the context of the Arab–Israeli dispute, or in Southeast Asia, if it were not for Soviet military forces. That is, I think, the principal problem that the United States is facing in relations with the Soviet Union. It is not only that the Soviet Union happens to be another ambitious superpower, but also that it is a superpower that relies on military force as its principal foreign policy instrument.

To what extent Gorbachev has changed this traditional reliance on military force is the central question of this inquiry. When Gorbachev became general secretary, some observers suggested initially that he was all style and little substance. I remember a major article by former President Nixon in *Time* magazine in which he said Americans are suckers for style. We are impressed with Gorbachev's freshness and his wife's preoccupation with Western lifestyles. We tend to forget that Nikita Khrushchev, in his baggy suit and peasant manners, was a rather formidable leader. One should not confuse style and substance. That is an appropriate warning. But if one looks at Gorbachev's foreign policy, one can see easily that there is more than a stylistic change. There is clearly some new substance to the Soviet foreign policy. The question is, what kind of substance and what does it mean for the United States?

On the one hand, Gorbachev quickly positioned himself as a champion of peace and arms control. His new disarmament initiative, in which he promised or suggested nothing short of total and complete nuclear disarmament, is well known. In the past every Soviet and American leader felt obliged to pay lip service to this beautiful dream: Joseph Stalin and Harry Truman; Brezhnev and Jimmy Carter; Gorbachev's predecessor, Konstantin Chernenko and Reagan. But it was primarily lip service—a general articulation of the great hope that one day the formidable nuclear genie would be put back into the bottle.

Gorbachev, on the other hand, has proposed a plan that is specific and complete: in three stages over fifteen years, all nuclear weapons are to be eliminated. During the first five-year stage, the United States and the Soviet Union would reduce their strategic and intermediate range nuclear missles by 50 percent. Just a short time ago the Soviets were insisting that before any agreement to reduce Soviet and U.S. missiles in Western Europe can be reached, the West must accept the Soviet Union's demand that it must be compensated for French and British nuclear forces. Now they say they are willing to permit the British and French to keep their nuclear forces as long as they do not upgrade them.

Gorbachev also says that he is willing to submit to on-site inspections. In the past, the Soviets rejected highly intrusive on-site inspections, and when U.S. negotiators demanded such inspections, the Soviets and their friends charged that the Americans were not serious about arms control. This new Soviet acceptance of the principle of on-site inspections is therefore a very interesting development.

To be sure, Gorbachev has indicated that the Soviet Union would not accept major reductions in strategic nuclear systems unless there was also progress in stopping Mr. Reagan's Strategic Defense Initiative. But here, too, there is some change. In the past the Soviets said there could be no progress on any nuclear issue unless Mr. Reagan stops SDI. Now the Soviets are saying there can be no progress on strategic arms control unless SDI is scrapped. But as far as an interim agreement on nuclear forces in Europe is concerned, it does not appear to be necessary to achieve progress on SDI. It is suggested that we could conclude an agreement on this issue today. (To the apparent surprise of the U.S. delegation at the Reykjavik summit, however, the Soviets again insisted on linking SDI and European nuclear forces. In March 1987 the Soviets reversed themselves and said that intermediate range missiles in Europe could be separated from SDI—editors' note.)

The new Soviet proposal to eliminate nuclear weapons is, from my point of view, a very forthright and creative Soviet concession. But how does it affect the United States? That is a very difficult question, because it is more a philosophical issue than something that strategic experts are entitled to handle. We must ask ourselves how comfortable we are with the current nuclear balance. On the one hand, of course, we are chained with the Soviets to the same doomsday machine. Everyone knows about nuclear winter. We have seen the television movie, "The Day After." Everyone knows that nuclear war would be an unmitigated, unthinkable, disaster.

On the other hand, for forty years the United States and the Soviet Union, despite so many conflicts and disagreements, have never gone to war. Indeed, they have not even engaged in a minor military skirmish. In terms of history and traditional progress in diplomacy, this is an enormous accomplishment, one that we owe in large part to nuclear weapons. Precisely because they are so horrible, nuclear weapons have been very helpful in maintaining peace.

This is the first consideration we must consider in evaluating Gorbachev's proposals. There is a second consideration. I know that for many people who do not follow strategic arms control discussions very closely, the idea of reducing nuclear weapons by 50 percent sounds appealing. But it has very little appeal to most strategic analysts, because it is of little military consequence. The fact remains that the United States and the Soviet Union could completely destroy each other and the rest of mankind with only 5 percent of their existing nuclear arsenals. And when I say 5 percent, I am not taking this figure from the top of my head but from very careful calculations by the USSR Academy of Sciences. We have built such an enormous nuclear overkill that we are really dealing with a great deal of nuclear fat. Cutting this fat may be very appealing, but it does not make very much difference militarily.

Of course, Gorbachev must know that eliminating all nuclear weapons is entirely unrealistic. Even without any on-site inspection, one can use satellites to count the numbers of strategic aircraft, missile launchers, and missile-carrying submarines on both sides. But how is one to know whether a peaceful-looking civilian ship is equipped with short-range cruise missiles, which can be hidden in the hold of the ship? Or are we to have Soviet and U.S. inspectors on every ship and give them access to every room and compartment?

One must also ask whether the United States would be willing to destroy all nuclear weapons and rely on Colonel Khadafy's common sense in not building his own and using them against the United States. And would the Soviet Union have much faith in the peaceful intentions of the Chinese or their other neighbors? As long as nuclear weapons can help people accomplish their objectives, there is no way to destroy them altogether. What Gorbachev has suggested are interesting steps in the direction of nuclear disarmament, but, unfortunately, the steps do not address the fundamental strategic situation.

Strategic analysts usually argue that counting nuclear weapons makes less sense than focusing on the kinds of weapons that are considered to be particularly dangerous or destabilizing. An example would be the so-called depressed trajectory submarine based-missiles, which are considered to be very dangerous for the simple reason that submarines can operate close to coastal territory and their missiles, which do not fly very high, have a short warning time. As a result they can be used to eliminate each other's national leadership and command control centers. That is why it is a priority for the United States in Geneva to find some way to control the development of these weapons. It would be easy to provide a short or a long list of other weapons that are dangerous and destabilizing. Unfortunately, Gorbachev's proposal does not deal with this qualitative issue. He has asked us to believe that reducing nuclear arsenals by 50 percent would be very meaningful. It certainly would be very dramatic. It would be a tremendous symbol, but as mentioned previously, it would make no difference militarily.

There is another concern that is even greater than those described above, namely, that both sides claim and seem to believe that nuclear war is inherently unwinnable, that a nuclear confrontation cannot be controlled, and accordingly, that a nuclear strike is not a rational policy tool. Thus there is a school of thought, both in the United States and in the Soviet Union, including the Soviet military, according to which we have wasted a great deal of effort and a great deal of money on nuclear forces while neglecting what really counts: our conventional nonnuclear forces. For many years it was almost gospel in Washington and Moscow that in terms of conventional weapons the Soviet Union was ahead of the United States and that the balance was changing even more in their favor. This view is increasingly questioned in the United States and the Soviet Union alike. In terms of numbers and assembly line capabilities, the Soviet Union is indeed far ahead of the United States. They can produce more tanks and aircraft, and, of course, they have many more soldiers in their armed forces. But the question of quality and technology makes the Soviets feel increasingly uncertain.

One dramatic event that made a great impression on Soviet leadership was the disaster encountered by the Syrian air force in June 1982, when it confronted the Israelis over the Bakaa Valley in Lebanon. During that air battle, the Israelis lost two planes, while the Syrians lost 85 of their Soviet-made aircraft. Neither of the Israeli planes was destroyed by the Syrian air force; both were destroyed by ground fire. The Soviets would argue that Soviet pilots are far superior to Syrian pilots. And the Syrians would complain that the Soviets have supplied them with so-called export models, which are usually of a previous, somewhat obsolete, generation. Both arguments may be at least partially true. Still, they do not quite explain the ratio of 85 against two. After this disaster, Soviet commanders, including the former chief of their general staff, Marshal Agarkov, began to discuss the need for upgrading Soviet conventional forces and for introducing new, sophisticated nonnuclear technologies. It was argued that the future battle is very likely going to be nonnuclear. The Soviet military leaders seem to be saying that "if we are chained together with the United States to the same doomsday machine, we are not likely to rely on nuclear weapons almost no matter what, so we have to build forces that are politically and militarily usable, that is, nonnuclear conventional forces." Gorbachev's proposal concerning nuclear weapons is very much in line with this kind of thinking—rely on those military forces that one can realistically use.

Is this good news for the United States? I am not sure that it is in the U.S. interest to embrace arms control proposals that would help the Soviet Union build usable military forces and compete with the United States effectively all over the globe. Of course, no Soviet proposal, like no U.S. proposal, can be assessed in isolation from other dimensions of foreign policy. If Gorbachev had delivered his breathtaking proposal at a time when Soviet foreign policy was becoming genuinely more moderate, I would say that it contained some interesting and encouraging elements and would urge its approval as an investment in a better tomorrow. But on the same day that we read about Gorbachev's nuclear proposal, we read also about the Soviet Union's decision to accelerate the construction of its second full-scale aircraft carrier. This second ship is a significant development, especially if the Soviets decide to build more such ships, since this is one area in which the United States currently enjoys a decisive military advantage. And we see no sign whatsoever of reduced investment in other Soviet conventional forces.

On the same day that Gorbachev delivered his arms control proposal, Soviet radio advised the government of Iran to conclude peace with Iraq, not in order to establish peace per se, but as the Soviet radio put it, in order to launch a decisive crusade against a common enemy—U.S. imperialism and Zionism. Everyone knows what the Soviet navy was doing around Libya while Gorbachev was delivering his proposal. While addressing a news conference in Washington, Jonas Savimbi, the leader of UNITA, the Angolan anti-Soviet guerrilla movement, made the case that since Gorbachev came to power, the Soviet intervention in Angola has increased in scope. The Soviets are supplying the pro-communist Angolan government with more sophisticated Soviet weapons, including modern aircraft and T-62 tanks. I have some difficulty evaluating Mr. Savimbi's charge, but from the little I know, it sounds quite plausible, and that is disturbing.

The Soviets under Gorbachev have become more assertive in their support of Libya, supplying them with SA-5 long-range anti-aircraft missiles. While these missiles are obsolete and would not be very effective against modern fighters and interceptors, they could help Colonel Khadafy to destroy civilian airliners or U.S. reconnaissance and AWAC-type aircraft. In addition, the Soviets have sent to Libya thousands of their military advisers.

These developments have taken place since Gorbachev came to power. When Konstantin Chernenko was in office, Khadafy wanted to visit the Soviet Union, and some preliminary announcements were made by both the Libyans and the Soviets. But the visit did not take place, because disagreements were far too great. After Chernenko's death, Khadafy finally travelled to Moscow, where he received red carpet treatment from Mr. Gorbachev. It seems that this development is more revealing of Gorbachev's intentions in making his nuclear arms proposals than is some other evidence.

When Konstantin Chernenko died, one world Communist leader was conspicuous by his absence at Mr. Chernenko's funeral: Fidel Castro. The reason Castro did not go to Moscow was allegedly because he felt that Chernenko had been too timid in confronting the United States in Central America and specifically in supporting the Sandinistas. Under Gorbachev Castro has had no reason to complain, because the Soviet commitment to Nicaragua has been upgraded considerably.

Afghanistan is another disturbing case. Under Gorbachev the Soviets brought 20,000 more troups into Afghanistan and launched two major new offensives. If in the past the Soviets were concerned essentially with controlling the major cities and highways, now they have begun to engage in large search-and-destroy missions, and they are willing to absorb higher casualties in the process. Recently the Chinese issued a statement explaining their reluctance to enter a nonaggression agreement with the Soviet Union, an agreement proposed by the Kremlin. The Chinese have explained that before signing such an agreement—one that would be highly symbolic and would inevitably create a great deal of euphoria in Moscow—they would expect the Soviets to display moderation on such questions as Afghanistan, Kampuchea, and of course, the presence of Soviet troops on the Chinese-Soviet border. The Chinese made it very clear that while Gorbachev expressed great interest in improving relations with China, he also made no concessions on any of these matters.

It is common knowledge that the Soviets are very interested in cultivating Japan, and Gorbachev's foreign minister, Eduard Shevardnadze, travelled to Tokyo in January, the first visit by a Soviet foreign minister in ten years. The Soviets are interested in prying the Japanese away from the United States and in reducing the Japanese military effort. Of course, they also want Japanese investment and technology. Yet on the contentious issue of the Northern territories, the four islands that were occupied by the Soviets at the end of World War II, the Soviets made no concessions whatsoever. Even the very fact that there is disagreement on this issue was not explicitly incorporated into the final communique, because the Soviets have refused to admit the existence of any conflict. We should be reminded that the Soviet-Japanese situation is very different from Japanese-U.S. territorial disputes after the war. Japan did not attack the Soviet Union. During World War II, Japan strictly observed its neutrality commitment as far as the Soviet Union was concerned. Yet at the end of the war, the Soviets violated their nonaggression agreement with Japan when they occupied these four islands.

What I am trying to suggest is this: under Mikhail Gorbachev the substance, not just the style, of Soviet foreign policy has changed. We are dealing with an impressive and creative man, one who is not dogmatic, a man who is willing to think about new and interesting approaches and who has improved the conduct of Soviet foreign policy considerably. What disappoints me somewhat is that in spite of some changes, he is pursuing essentially the same old Soviet objectives, relying essentially on the same time-tested Soviet policy tool, namely, military force.

This raises another fundamental question, the last one I want to discuss briefly before concluding. What are U.S. interests in relation to the Soviet Union, and particularly, what should be the U.S. approach to Gorbachev's domestic reforms? I have lived in the United States for thirteen years, and I am always impressed by and delighted with U.S. optimism and generosity in thinking about international relations. The trouble with this wonderful approach, which is very appealing and which makes the United States a wonderful country to live in, is that it is rather divorced from international reality. For instance, I just read in a major weekly a quote from a leading U.S. Sovietologist, who said, "Unfortunately, there is no evidence that Mr. Gorbachev, indeed, is capable of restructuring the Soviet economy." I do not disagree with that observation, but what intrigued me was why it should be unfortunate? Why is it unfortunate if your principal military rival may not be able to revive his economy? One must ask what is the basic nature of U.S. and Soviet relations? If our problems with the Soviet Union are primarily the result of some unfortunate misunderstanding, of some kind of paranoia or distrust, then, of course, we should wish them well, hope that they will become fat communists, build bridges and try to bribe them into good behavior. But if we believe, as de Tocqueville observed more than a century ago, that Russia and the United States are two great powers, almost structurally bound to compete with each other—that was, of course, before Russia became Communist—if they both have global interests, global visions, and are rather intolerant of each other, and if they have different goals and objectives, then one may assume that the Soviet-U.S. rivalry cannot be resolved. It can only be managed. That may be a new experience for the United States. But that is what world history is all about. History does not offer any resolution. It is a continuing drama, in which one moves from one challenge to another. After each success, one always encounters a new setback.

If that is one's view of international relations and history and one's view of relations with the Soviet Union, if one believes that as long as they are what they are, and as long as the United States has global interests to protect and the determination to protect them, if one believes that the relationship is going to be dominated by rivalry, then one has to ask: how much do we want to help the Soviet Union to reform itself economically and to become, accordingly, more powerful militarily?

Some people are suggesting—and Gorbachev is making this case all the time—that because of his preoccupation with the Soviet economy, he has to spend less on defense. From Russian history we learn that the Russians usually introduce major reforms after suffering some military defeats and in order to improve their armed forces. The same Sovietologist whom I just cited compared Gorbachev with Peter the Great. I hope that is an exaggeration, because if that is true, neighbors of the Soviet Union are in trouble. And in the present global nuclear age, everybody is everybody's neighbor.

Even more importantly, we should not forget that in the short run, Gorbachev's arms control has nothing to do with Soviet reductions in military spending. First of all, one has to think about strategic and intermediate range nuclear forces. According to the CIA—and this happens to be a rather noncontroversial estimate—the Soviets do not spend more than eight to ten percent of their overall military budget on their strategic and intermediate range nuclear forces. This means that even a ten to fifteen percent reduction in spending on their strategic forces is not economically meaningful and cannot be dictated by economic considerations. Secondly, who told us that arms control results in decreased defense spending? Does anyone think the Soviets would spend less if they reduced the numbers of their nuclear weapons? Absolutely not. The greatest costs, as far as keeping these weapons is concerned, are maintenance costs, which are fairly low in the Soviet case. On the other hand, dismantling these weapons, introducing sophisticated verification procedures, and, most importantly, proceeding with a restructuring of Soviet forces from land-based to sea-based deterrence, which would be required by this kind of arms control, would cost the Soviets more in the short run. The fact that Gorbachev wants to save money has nothing to do with his nuclear arms control proposal.

Of fundamental importance in any assessment of Soviet intentions is what appears to be a consensus among the Soviet elite, including the military leadership, that the Soviet Union has to rely less on nuclear forces. I do not think there is any kind of consensus that the Soviet Union has to rely less on military power. What the Soviet leaders are talking about is not genuine, comprehensive disarmament, but essentially changing their priorities, rechanneling their efforts and their resources into conventional forces. I am not quite sure that that is very much in the U.S. interest.

In closing, I should like to suggest that it is going to be more exciting to deal with Gorbachev than with his predecessors. He has already proved that he is a formidable rival, and perhaps more accommodating in areas of mutual interest where Soviet and U.S. interests overlap. In the past it was difficult to cooperate with the Soviets, because their dogmatic leaders would say "nyet," even when it was not in their best interest. Now we have a man in the Kremlin who knows how to say "yes" when it is in their basic interest. As a result we will probably be able to reach some limited arms control agreeements. We will probably have some mutual crisis stability centers in Moscow and Washington. We will probably have more trade, more cultural exchanges, and more contact in other areas. This is reassuring to the extent that we are dealing with another nuclear power, and it is only civilized to build shock absorbers to make our rivalry somewhat less explosive. But I have no impression whatsoever that Gorbachev's changes will abolish or reduce our rivalry per se. The excitement surrounding Gorbachev may not be with respect to his arms control proposals, but, unfortunately, about his actions that are much less benign, such as those in Libya, Nicaragua, and Angola.

Unfortunately, I must conclude with the reminder that weapons do not produce wars, situations produce wars. If Mr. Gorbachev reduces weapons but becomes more assertive in crisis situations, we are going to have to be very careful in dealing with our Soviet partner, who is, simultaneously, our Soviet adversary.

NOTES

1. V. N. Lamodorfa, *Dnevnik* (Moskva: Gosudarstvennoye Izdatel'stvo, 1926), p. 215.
2. S. Yn. Witte; *Vospominaniya*, V. 3 (Moskva: Izdatel'stvo Sotsialnoekonomicheskoi Literatury, 1960), pp. 254–55.

5 Gorbachev's Economic Prescriptions: A Preliminary Analysis

John P. Hardt and Jean Farneth Boone

In the following essay, John P. Hardt and Jean Farneth Boone address the question of the Soviet economy, with its numerous shortcomings and failings, and analyze what measures Gorbachev and his lieutenants have proposed or actually implemented to revive or transform the economy, part of their quest to find the "formula for economic success." Hardt and Boone cite three different prescriptions suggested by Gorbachev and his associates at the 27th Party Congress: renewal of centralized planning and "mobilization;" "intensification;" and a Soviet "technological information revolution." While considering potential effects on a host of component issues such as investment, industry, agriculture, personnel, bureaucratic organization, and so on, they also discuss the complicated question of the "human factor" in policy formulation.

Hardt and Boone take issue with Simes' tentative analysis of the interrelationship of economic health and military power (or the willingness or perceived need to use the latter). Whereas Simes suggested the possibility of a strong economy's resulting in an even stronger military, Hardt and Boone conclude that the Soviet Union "could be a more challenging adversary, although not necessarily more threatening in military terms." They suggest that if Gorbachev fails to revive the economy, the inclination to use military force to prove great power status might be enhanced.

THE ECONOMIC PLAN

Since taking power in 1985, Mikhail Gorbachev has focused on the ailing Soviet economy as one of his prime concerns. Throughout his five and a half hour speech at the 27th Party Congress in Moscow, and in other speeches given by his lieutenants, Gorbachev has provided elements of at least three different prescriptions for the economy: (1) renewal of centralized planning and mobilization; (2) intensification; and (3) technological information revolution.

Renewal of Centralized Planning and Mobilization

A high growth rate, approaching that of the Stalinist command economy, must be regained in short order to meet the demands of competing claimants for scarce resources: "guns," "growth," and "butter." For this task of energizing the economy, Gorbachev has purged most of the old economic bureaucracy of Leonid Brezhnev and has brought in his own "efficient technocrats" under a new work ethic—one that requires "workaholics" not "alcoholics," and "productivity and participation" not "cronyism and corruption." From the enactment of this prescription the economy is to grow at a rate of over four percent per annum (twice the recent rate), with output doubling by the turn of the century under Gorbachev's Fifteen Year Plan (1986-2000).[1] Centralized planning is to be enhanced using Lenin's "commanding heights" as the model—more control over long-range planning will be held by the responsible political leaders at the top, while responsibility for day-to-day decision making will be decentralized to farms and factories.

Output did not increase in 1985 under Gorbachev as expected. Industrial growth was about the same as in 1983/84, oil production was down, and agricultural growth continued to decline, although the grain harvest was up. With regard to growth rates, the annual plan for 1986, the 12th Five Year Plan (1986-1990), and the Fifteen Year Plan to the year 2000 were not consistent, and Prime Minister Nikolai Ryzhkov's discussion at the Congress did not clear up all the ambiguities. The growth projections are increasingly ambitious: The average annual growth for Net Material Product is 3.8 percent for 1986–1990, 4.7 percent for 1991–1995, and 5.7 percent in 1996–2000. How will this ambitious growth be achieved?

Investment. Agriculture, energy, and machine building all are to have more investment. But the sharp rise in investment planned in 1986 (7.6 percent) seems inconsistent with the overall plan for 1986–1990 (3.5 to 4 percent per year). Moreover, investment in energy seems high for coal and oil and low for gas. It is not clear where investment for machine building will come from and what sectors will be crowded out. Given the substantial increase in allocations planned for investment and consumption, the inference is that defense could be squeezed, especially military procurement. Will sharply increased equipment and machine imports from CMEA (Council for Mutual Economic Assistance, the Eastern European counterpart to the European Economic Community) and the West make up the shortfall in investment resources? The Soviets are pressing for higher quality imports from Eastern Europe to meet their rising requirements for machinery and quality consumer goods. But how much more they will squeeze Eastern Europe is not clear.

Increased imports of machinery from the West, including the United States, are being discussed, but with falling income from oil sales, the Soviets must find other ways to balance trade, namely, increase debt, use hard currency reserves (currently $10 billion, mainly in Western banks),[2] or increase exports of oil, gas, and other resources. Some analysts estimate that the Soviets lost $3–4 billion in oil export revenue in 1985, and could lose $5–7 billion in 1986.[3] According to Wharton, gold sales might be increased by $2–3 billion over the next five years, without drastically reducing reserves, to improve the balance of payments.[4] Currently, the Soviet debt service ratio is estimated at 20 percent; if the Soviets choose to increase Western borrowing to meet oil earnings shortfall, the debt service ratio could rise even higher by 1990.[5] Another possible strategy could include reduced aid and loans to developing countries; in fact, Gorbachev indicated in his Party Congress speech that these LDC (Less Developed Countries) clients must find ways to become more self-sufficient. The evidence for the moment on expanding Western trade is that the Soviets are carefully assessing their options before commitment; they may also be waiting for better balance of payments news before committing large orders to the West.

Personnel. The infusion of new personnel and some streamlining of the economic bureaucracy appear to be important elements in energizing the economy to meet growth goals. Turnover within the party leadership since Gorbachev assumed power has been extensive: the Politburo now includes only three (of twelve) members not appointed by either Gorbachev or his mentor, Yuri Andropov; the party Secretariat of eleven includes seven Gorbachev appointees (and Gorbachev himself); more than half the Central Committee department heads have been appointed in the last year; and at the 27th Party Congress, about 40 percent of the membership of the Central Committee was replaced.

The "personnel weapon" has been used extensively both to strengthen support within the party for Gorbachev's policies and to bring a more experienced, technocratic cadre into leadership positions. Still, despite the widespread turnover, there were indications throughout the Congress of some continued resistance to Gorbachev's initiatives.

Bureaucratic organization. To strengthen the central economic ministries but narrow their focus from "operational management" to long-range structural planning, several super-ministries have been created: the State Agro-Industrial Committee, which merged five agricultural ministries and a committee, a Machine-Building Bureau that spans several industries, and a new energy "super-ministry." In the case of agriculture, this centralization of planning involves more horizontal coordination, an emphasis on agricultural strategy at a higher political level, and more decentralization of decision making and authority to the regions and individual collectives.[6] Gorbachev has used the creation of the new State Agro-Industrial Committee to eliminate most of the top government agricultural officials and to establish a new team that includes two of his former associates from Stavropol: his longtime Stavropol deputy and successor as *kray* (district) first secretary, V. S. Murakhovskiy, who became chairman and first deputy premier; and Lenin Agricultural Academy President A. A. Nikonov, head of the Stavropol Agricultural Institute while Gorbachev was *kray* first secretary, who became a deputy chairman. Another agricultural official from neighboring Krasnodar, G. A. Romanenko, was also made a deputy chairman of the new committee. Romanenko has headed the Krasnodar Agricultural Institute since his promotion from deputy director in mid-1985. Significantly, the ministry mergers have not simply combined the bureaucracies into a still larger, more inert bureaucracy, but rather have required a reduction in force, reportedly leading to the temporary unemployment of many and even the payment of unemployment benefits, an unprecedented occurrence. Whether such a strategy applied throughout the economy will be acceptable and achievable, given the political and social questions it raises, remains to be seen. Job security is still considered a right by manager and worker alike. If the process is successful, the creation of super-ministries or commissions for foreign trade and other key sectors is projected.

Intensification: A Soviet Economic Miracle

Capturing the essence of the Western "economic miracles," Gorbachev wants to create a more efficient economy, one that will use material and human resources better and will generate output that approaches the world level of quality. This prescription takes as its model the transformation of the post-war Western industrial economies in which efficient technological systems were introduced to increase significantly the productivity of energy, agricultural resources, manpower, and other inputs to production. The rationale is clear for replacing the extensive, albeit wasteful, system with processes that show a modicum of efficiency and quality. As Gorbachev noted in his speech at the Party Congress: "A national economy which possesses enormous resources has run up against a shortage of them." Thus,

1. The Soviet Union, the world's largest producer of energy, must now use two to three times more energy than the leading Western industrial countries to achieve the same degree of economic growth;

output of oil, gas, and coal is therefore not sufficient to meet domestic and export needs.
2. The world's largest producer of wheat loses so much of its harvest from field to mill that it has become a major importer of grain.
3. One of the world's most populous nations finds itself short of labor—especially short of Great Russians, who have become a minority in the multinational state—due to low labor productivity and inefficient use of human resources.

To utilize energy and labor more effectively, to improve the storage and distribution of grain crops, and to produce higher quality products for consumption and export, Gorbachev must shift the economy from its "extensive" growth plan (stressing increases in the quantity of factors of production) to an "intensive" one (stressing increases in the efficiency of these factors). Concentrating on replacement investment to improve capital efficiency and on effective incentives to raise labor productivity, he intends to reduce what is perceived as waste throughout the system. Gorbachev's plan calls for sharply increased investment in machinery to modernize hundreds of old industrial plants, as well as improvement in the economic infrastructure from field and factory to market.

For "the human factor"—improved productivity of labor and management—the task of "intensification" is more complex. Incentive systems must be introduced that will be perceived as fair and yet adequate to overcome the cynical, unproductive environment created by the system of guaranteed job security. For incentives to be effective, privilege must be replaced by performance; reward based on government or party rank must be supplanted by the opportunity to "work up to one's full potential." Those who are successful under this new incentive system need to be able to use their rubles to assure themselves of better housing, better transportation, and a better diet. The unsuccessful must be encouraged and motivated by discipline and education. Thus, penalties for being drunk at work are now said to include heavy fines and loss of access to priority housing, annual leave for summer vacations, and scarce quality goods.[7] Gorbachev's exhortations for this kind of incentive strategy might appeal to a planner in post-World War II Japan or South Korea—one can imagine that even Henry Ford would feel comfortable with the rhetoric of this work-ethic environment. Nevertheless, increased productivity through such a materialistic incentive system is now integral to the success of Soviet growth plans.

Industrial renovation. Intensification is to bring higher rates of industrial growth than were achieved in the past. According to Gorbachev, by the end of the century labor productivity will rise 2.3 to 2.5 times, the energy-output ratio of national income will be reduced by two-sevenths, and metal consumption will be nearly halved. Investment concentration on plant renovation seems to be a key part of the strategy, together with stepped-up machinery output. A special commission on restructuring the economy, headed by Gosplan Chairman N. Talyzin was set up at the Party Congress, presumably to develop a more detailed intensification plan. It seems that over 400 plants are now on the list for restructuring, renovation, and updating. Specific examples run a wide gamut: AZLIK (Moskvich, auto); VAZ (Zhugili, auto); Svobeda (perfumes); Bolshevitkhi (clothes); Likhachev (autos); Shegohod' (shoes).[8] The priority given to machine building seems to have brought about a shift away from large-scale investment projects, including the Baikal Amur (BAM) projects in East Siberia (as differentiated from the BAM railroad) and the water diversion project, Sibaral Canal, for Central Asia.

The retooling of industries is designed to enhance overall economic efficiency, and Gorbachev claims that it will save annually the labor of about twelve million people and over 100 million metric tons of fuel. To achieve these ambitious goals, 1.8 times more capital investment will be allocated to renovation of machine building industries than in the preceding 5 years. Questions remain, however, as to whether additional investment funds will be available, according to plan, as well as whether the Soviet machine-building and construction sectors would be able to absorb effectively such massive infusions of investment. Furthermore, as Prime Minister Ryzhkov recognized in his speech at the Party Congress, it will take ten years just to halt the decline in capital efficiency; only after the return on capital is stabilized—in "the first half of the nineties"—will this capital efficiency indicator actually begin to grow.

Agricultural investment and reform. A high rate of investment in the agricultural sector—28 percent of the total (possibly rising to one third, according to Prime Minister Ryzhkov's Congress speech)—is planned to continue. From this investment the Soviets expect results to include sharp reductions in harvest losses, improved food processing, increased local responsibility, and improved infrastructure—rural housing, transport, roads, and storage, all supported by local funds. As one example of what can be achieved, Gorbachev stated at the Party Congress that the use of the new DON-1500 combine harvester will alone reduce the stock of grain harvesting machines, disengage about 400,000 machine operators, and reduce the losses of grain by millions of metric tons.

Gorbachev has indicated that farm units, including the family, may gain responsibility and have rights to market a substantial share of their output. The greater decentralization of agriculture is to be achieved by a return to a "food tax," a principal tool of the New Economic Policy under Lenin. Under this program as described by Gorbachev at the Party Congress, agricultural enterprises and agricultural regions will be free to market independently any produce above the quota—a tax in kind—they must deliver to the state, "thereby raising their interest in and responsibility for the final results." In the text of Lenin's proposal to the Politburo and the decree published in 1921, the concept is clearly articulated that agricultural production could be increased by guaranteeing to the individual peasant family freedom to dispose of its harvest above the tax in kind, and freedom and security in the tenure of their land.[9] In the discussion of the decree, the questions of leasing of land and use of hired labor were debated but not resolved. These revolutionary changes in Soviet agriculture, proposed in 1921 and referred to by Gorbachev and his advisers, were never initiated because 1921 was a poor crop year—indeed a year of famine. Although Lenin's plan was never fully implemented, Gorbachev directly referred to the Leninist precedent. The chairman of the USSR State Agro-Industrial Committee, in discussing the tax in kind, went even further than Gorbachev when he stated in his speech at the Party Congress that "the socialist market must play an important role in increasing the volume and improving the quality of output."

The human factor. The increase in labor productivity is critical for intensification and a key to all output goals. Prime Minister Ryzhkov noted that labor resources will increase by only 3.2 million persons over the next five years, whereas it would require 22 million additional persons to achieve Soviet growth goals at current levels of productivity. Thus, industrial labor productivity must rise from 3.1 percent annual growth in 1981–1985 to 8.8 percent by 2000. According to Ryzhkov at the Party Congress, two thirds of this increase will result from "assimilation of new machinery and technology." Presumably, the remaining third will come from the "human factor."

As part of the incentive to labor, real income is to increase 1.6 to 1.8 times over the 15-year period; however, as assumption that labor will overcome past inertia, including drunkenness, is based not only on higher incomes but also on a variety of changes ranging from enhanced discipline to a significant range of rewards. Among the rewards could be increased availability of consumer services. At the Party Congress Gorbachev emphasized "services connected with aiding housework, the provision of services and amenities for and repair of flats, tourism, and vehicle servicing—the demand for which is growing particularly rapidly." Several officials have indicated that those people released from industry as a result of automation and increased labor productivity could be used to develop the service sector. Ryzhkov suggested that all *new* labor resources be channelled into the nonproduction sphere—education, public health, and other services. Gorbachev, too, stressed the need for improved public health care, noting in his speech that "we must satisfy as soon as possible the population's requirements for high-quality curative, preventive, and medicinal help and in all geographical areas. . . . [O]f course, considerable funds will be required, and we shall have to find them."

Important incentives for labor will also include increased meat availability (production to reach 21 million tons annually) and housing availability (565–570 million square meters of housing to be constructed during the 12th Five Year Plan, and individual housing to be available for everyone by the end of the century). As part of the effort to increase the population's access to quality goods, the privileged status of the party elite is apparently open for discussion, including the right to use special, well stocked stores—a subject never before discussed publicly.

It may be difficult to provide a sufficient number of needed, effective incentives exclusively by increasing the availability of quality goods. But better services, more equity, the opportunity for greater participation, and the feeling that the leadership cares may all be important in improving morale. In his Party Congress speech, Moscow party boss Boris Yeltsin struck an interesting theme for Moscow: "to make the city cleaner, more civilized, more comfortable; to struggle for the honor and dignity of Muscovites."

A Soviet Technological Information Revolution

Computer applications, micro-electronics, the use of lasers and robotics—all are part of the dramatic change occurring in the economies of the Western industrial nations. Gorbachev has stressed repeatedly that the Soviet Union must not fall further behind in this new frontier of science, technology, and economic development. For the Soviet Union, the serious threat of the Strategic Defense Initiative (SDI) may be in its technological message. Civilian technological dynamism drives our SDI research programs and, whether or not the military defense vision of President Reagan is credible or attainable, its technological components are. Thus, SDI symbolizes a further, potentially serious erosion of Soviet claims to being an economic superpower. Because of its deteriorating economic base, the Soviet Union may become a more technologically inferior military power. Gorbachev may know that he needs an open, dynamic, and innovative scientific and technological community—one that can see its fruits translated into operational systems—but if he recognizes the need, he has not yet presented the program for addressing it. His speeches persist in suggesting that more resources in a centralized science and technology system can provide improved results.

It is possible that the current upsurge in military-industrial espionage reflects a perceived need to catch up technologically. In taking this approach, however, the Soviets miss serving their long-term economic requirement for a broad, modern, and technologically dynamic research and development establishment of their own.

While complaining in his Party Congress speech about the "number of scientific discoveries and major inventions which do not find their practical application for years, sometimes for decades," Gorbachev did not propose any detailed program for improving the links between research and production, other than "coordinating material incentives of scientific collectives and individual workers with their real contribution to resolving scientific and technical problems." The automation and mechanization of industry are strongly emphasized—the number of industrial robots is to treble during the next five years, the use of "progressive technologies" is to increase by 50 to 100 percent and "mass assimilation" of computer technology is to take place. While an intellectually open, interconnected scientific research community is most critical and important, computer education, information networks for industry, transportation, health care services, and other sectors are also integral elements in a successful technological revolution.

Furthermore, Gorbachev's economy, if it is to make progress in this new technological revolution, must at least selectively join the world market. Recognizing this, Gorbachev called again at the 27th Party Congress for controlled interdependence with the West. Reform of the Soviet foreign economic institutions, as Gorbachev's economic lieutenant, Prime Minister Ryzhkov, suggested in his Party Congress speech, must promote direct contact and cooperation between Soviet enterprises and those of their trading partners in Eastern Europe and the West. In this way, noncompetitive enterprises can be renovated and new technologies developed.

Western imports may play a significant role in the planned technological progress of the Soviet economy. Ryzhkov noted that the USSR sees "considerable potentialities" for cooperation with developed capitalist states, including all kinds of relations—"commercial, scientific, technical, finance, and credits."

In his Party Congress speech, Ryzhkov called for reorganizing Soviet foreign trade institutions and opening relations with the West, implying a green light for joint ventures.[10]

GORBACHEV'S RADICAL REFORM REQUIRES INSTITUTIONAL SURGERY

There is a logic to proceeding on all of Gorbachev's prescriptions for his ailing economy, and yet these prescriptions are not necessarily compatible, and their implementation could raise serious dilemmas for the leadership. Energizing and mobilizing the centralized planning system (prescription no. 1) could bring some improvement in the short run, but prescriptions nos. 2 and 3 will require fundamental changes in the economic system that can only be fully implemented over a longer period of time—perhaps through the end of the century. Given this two-stage process—short-term mobilization, followed by more radical reform—Gorbachev's lack of specificity on long-range programs may be understandable. However, if the economy is successfully mobilized for higher growth and there is a perception that the economy's problems are solved, significant reform may seem politically postponable. If all three are nonetheless eventually pursued, the imperatives of the intensification and the technological-information prescriptions suggest that institutional and systemic surgery will be needed and will *not* be optional.

Although neither Gorbachev nor Ryzhkov developed a detailed blueprint of change, despite statements that "we cannot limit ourselves to partial improvements," Gorbachev's speech contained many of the code phrases signalling the type of change required and legitimizing the commitment of many in his administration to go forward with reform both over the short and long term:

1. Relevance of prices ("Prices are to become an active tool of economic and social policy"; a first step may be physical quotas or rationing of scarce labor and energy inputs and bonuses for outputs that meet world market standards);
2. Decentralization of agricultural decision making on planting, culti-

vation, and marketing to the family unit ("Subcontracting and the piece-work system at the team level among work units and families will become more widespread");
3. Right of industrial enterprises to sell many of their own products ("Enterprises . . . should be given the right to independently market above-plan output, unused raw and manufactured materials and equipment");
4. Legalization or co-option of the informal or illegal services sector ("Decisive measures must be adopted to eliminate marked imbalances between demand for services and their supply").

The ministerial economic bureaucracy is clearly the primary target of the required institutional reform. Gorbachev, like his counterpart in Washington, is fighting the bureaucrats in his capital city. Notably, at the Party Congress, Gorbachev's new head of the Moscow party organization, Boris Yeltsin, even attacked the party bureaucracy directly, asking, "Why, even now, is the demand for radical changes getting stuck in the inert layers of time-servers who possess party cards?"

Apparently a coherent, comprehensive strategy for reforming the governmental and party economic bureaucracies, one that would provide for both more effective central planning and decentralized management, has not yet been worked out, especially for the technological-information revolution. Possibly it is too early to begin detailed implementation. Perhaps Gorbachev does not yet see the full requirements for economic change. Or it may be that full-scale institutional change will await establishment of a more solid political base, particularly the replacement of the remaining Brezhnev holdovers, D. Kunayev and V. Shcherbitsky—party bosses in Kazakhstan and the Ukraine, respectively. (Kunayev was replaced by G. Kolbin in December 1986—editors' note.)

The assurance of solid political support is critical before proceeding, since movement toward a price system for effective planning and toward profitability criteria for effective management would reduce the economic rights, authority, and privileges of the party and government bureaucracies. A major restructuring of the ministerial system to narrow management at the center and revision of the *nomenklatura* system that ensures party control of personnel privileges and rewards at all levels of the economy are both essential for successful reform, but some would say they are politically impossible.

Many questions remain unresolved. Abel Aganbegyan, a reform-minded economist and leading adviser to Gorbachev, spelled out the gaps in the economic strategy during a post-Congress conference: How will retail prices be made more realistic? How will the leadership close or restructure unprofitable enterprises? What will be done with manual workers replaced by machines? He noted, too, that the massive subsidies for bread, meat, and milk must be reduced if retail prices are to be rationalized (according to a pre-Congress Gorbachev speech at Tselinograd, subsidies for meat alone now cost 20 billion rubles per year).[11] Volgograd party official V. I. Kalashnikov called for an increase in food prices to close the subsidy gap in his speech to the Congress. But reduction of subsidies would pose a direct challenge to the equally important need to support consumption and increase living standards. These dilemmas, among others, will have to be faced if reform proceeds over the long term.

While many specialists inside and outside the Soviet Union carefully studying Gorbachev's speeches and programs might agree that Gorbachev's rhetoric implies an acceptance of the need for and the promise of change, they would say that this is where he stops, that the rhetoric of radical reform will not be followed with action. Still, he has raised expectations. His speeches and actions may have been as provocative to the Soviet establishment and citizens as Khrushchev's de-Stalinization speech thirty years ago at the 20th Party Congress, which created a momentum that carried forward through the 22nd Congress in 1961. For criticism of party leaders and the *nomenklatura* system as far-reaching as those found in Yeltsin's speech, one would have to go back to the 15th Party Congress in 1927. But given the political risk of carrying out a truly "radical reform," some would argue that Gorbachev might, perhaps at the next party congress in 1991, simply declare economic victory with an energized economy and stop, never going beyond "mobilization" and some intensification toward comprehensive reform. If he should take this path, however, even the modest success of mobilization—revival of the Soviet spirit, hopes, and expectations—could be dashed and a very cynical backlash could follow. Then Yeltsin's criticism of the past would again be relevant: the party once again identified serious problems, posed as "miracle workers," but did nothing to bring about necessary changes. Furthermore, it would mean that the USSR would not be able to compete with the technological challenge of SDI.

Regardless of whether Gorbachev is a tactician or a strategist, there are objective factors that seem likely to press him forward to adopt, rationalize, and proceed on all three economic prescriptions:

1. The rising expectations of the intellectual elite and the populace, "the human factor," including the introduction of fair and stimulating incentive systems, is a genie that will not easily go back into the bottle, and without incentives, necessary improvement in labor productivity is not likely to occur.
2. The technological competition with the United States and other Western industrial countries has such profound implications for Soviet political, economic, and military power that the challenge must rationally be met, not avoided. In this all the power holders in the party, military, and police have a stake. The populace, too, could be stirred by the patriotic appeal for enhancing the nation's power status.
3. The opening of the economy to the world market, effectively utilizing imported Western technology, cannot be avoided or reversed without heavy costs and is essential for improving the efficiency and quality of Soviet output.

FORMULA FOR ECONOMIC SUCCESS

Given Gorbachev's objectives for economic performance from now until the end of the century and the broadly defined prescriptions that emerged from the Party Congress, a range of specific reform measures, from short-term adjustments to radical institutional change, may be included on the menu from which Gorbachev will draw over time. Some elements of change have already been implemented. Others were articulated at the Congress but have not yet been given administrative form. Still more far-reaching proposals are being debated within the economic and scientific communities. The most fundamental aspects of systemic change may not yet be open for discussion, but would follow logically in a comprehensive progression of change. Which elements from this range will Gorbachev choose? How far will he want or be able to carry the process of reform? While the Party Congress itself did not provide the answers to these questions, they will become more evident as the Gorbachev era unfolds. For each of the three prescriptions described at the beginning of this chapter, one could look for a progressive formula for success, a checklist of dilemmas to be resolved and obstacles overcome, that will indicate Gorbachev's path as it is forged between now and the end of the century. In this way we might assess the seriousness of Gorbachev's commitment, the constraints that may inhibit his progress, and his prospects for success.

Renewal of Centralized Planning and Mobilization

1. A comprehensive application of the "commanding heights" concept could be achieved with a thorough elevation of planning to horizontally integrated units involving sectors, such as machine building, agriculture, and energy, with a top party leader directly responsible to the general secretary for the implementation of Gorbachev's strategy. This clearer delineation of planning and policy responsibility provides the basis for decentralization of management to the enterprises and streamlining of the ministerial system. A process apparently well underway, it could be carried out throughout all sectors of the economy, including defense, with potentially significant results. The agricultural sector, already reorganized, could show marked improvement in performance if external factors—particularly weather—are positive. Success here could then provide impetus for changes in other sectors.
    - Energizing the system requires a constant reassessment of performance against tasks, not a one-shot effort. As Yeltsin noted, leaders should be held accountable for delivering on their promises. If they do not meet the test of achievement, they should suffer the consequences—from the top ranks to the operating level. As Gorbachev's strategy moves through its various stages from energizing to radical reform, the process of constant reappraisal would

be necessary—a Phoenix principle. One might then expect the new economic lieutenants implementing the Gorbachev renewal to be up or out depending on their ability to adjust and be successful.
- Pressure for more growth needs to be tied to increased efficiency and high quality. The introduction of quality control criteria for attaining world standards could serve to guard against a reemergence of gross output measures as the key success indicator.
- In mobilizing resources to serve the needs of industrial modernization and agricultural improvement, the leadership will need to consider the orderly economic progress of deferred or stretched-out programs. The costs of deferment may be minimized by restricting new starts in lower priority areas and providing priority for projects underway, for example, making the Baikal-Amur railroad fully operative and completing plants in the priority lists for modernization.

Intensification

The intensification program for industrial modernization is key to reducing the required inputs of labor and materials and increasing the quality of output toward world norms. It will require, however, a multi-faceted approach affecting all aspects of the economy and is likely to require a long-term effort to be fully effective. In addressing the "human factor," agricultural reform, and industrial revolution, a variety of measures have been or could be taken that carry with them varying degrees of cost and political risk.

1. Improved labor productivity: the human factor.
   - Increasing services may be one of the less difficult and costly options available to the leadership for stimulating worker motivation and productivity. Services could be improved and quality enhanced by legalizing or formalizing the informal economy, a step not requiring new resources. More workers may be assigned to services. Gorbachev suggested, for example, that pensioners could provide services and produce consumer goods "on a cooperative as well as on a personal and family basis." Increasing the accountability of the leadership to the population was another theme sounded, particularly by Yeltsin, at the Party Congress. Top lead-

ership, local soviets and party units could all be pressured to monitor delivery of services more carefully. A sense of concern expressed by leaders in the interests of cities they oversee might help reverse the cynicism produced by the privileges now enjoyed by the party elite. Thus leaders could promote the feeling among the people that they care, that the system is more equitable, rather than encouraging the feeling that they take all the quality goods and leave the rest for the "people." Unlike other means of improving productivity, some gains along this line could be achieved without substantial costs or new resources and could have an important impact on worker morale.

- In addition to improved services, increased availability of goods—especially meat and other quality food, reliable autos, and housing and facilities—would also be required to provide a stimulus for more productivity. The changes in agriculture, together with good weather and the stimulation of consumer goods industries, might provide more attractive goods. It will take some time, however, for goods availability and quality to increase, since industrial renovation will have to be implemented first. Similarly, a reduction of the pervasive system of privilege might release more quality goods for the productive worker and manager but will likely be constrained by party opposition. Although this idea is open for discussion, as evidenced by Yeltsin's speech, it is very controversial—as suggested by Ligachev's subsequent comments that party privileges are deserved. (See also pp. 116 and 145 for a discussion of this incident—editors' note.) Finally, increased imports from CMEA countries and elsewhere could also be used to expand the quality and selection on the shelves.

- Increased availability of machinery may be a substantial source of increases in labor productivity. Prime Minister Ryzhkov indicated that two thirds of the increase might come from new machinery and technology. Of course this goal, like that of increasing goods, requires successful investment in machine building to occur first, before labor productivity gains can be made.

- Revision of the wage system and income policy may be made to provide more to the most productive. Gorbachev stated in his speech that "the state's policy in the sphere of wages should ensure that wages are strictly dependent upon the quantity and quality of labor." To strengthen this link, he proposed that wage and salary increases come out of the funds earned by the enterprises themselves. Making foreign goods available to the most productive workers may be an additional stimulus.

Economic Prescriptions / 91

- The campaign against corruption and unearned income is the corollary to the revised wage system. Corruption standards must be applied to the top leadership as well.
- Worker participation could be increased as an incentive by encouraging socialist democracy in enforcing discipline, controlling alcoholism, and monitoring wage systems. Workers may also have a voice in choice of managers. According to Gorbachev, "it is evidently advisable to extend the appointment-by-election process to all team leaders, and then gradually to certain other categories of managerial staff of enterprise."

2. Decentralization and incentives in agriculture.
   - The creation of the new State Agro-Industrial Committee establishes a power base for Gorbachev's lieutenants to implement decentralization. This ministerial reorganization is the first step in what Gorbachev recognizes as a multi-stage effort to place agriculture under workable economic norms: "The USSR State Agro-Industrial Committee sets the following task: to transfer in the next two years basically all *kolkhozes* [collective farms] and *sovkhozes* [state farms] to complete financial autonomy.... We understand that much work remains to be done to improve economic management and the efficient utilization of levers like prices, profits, and profitability."
   - V. Murakhovskiy, the head of the "super ministry," may implement the concept of Lenin's "food tax" as described at the Party Congress. This would involve giving authority to the local unit (the family) to make planting decisions, control distribution and marketing of part of the harvest, and retain profits resulting from revenue in excess of costs. If weather is average or good, it might be expected that the "food tax experiment" would be applied first to the South, given the fact that Gorbachev and his lieutenant came from Krasnodar, Stavropol, and environs. Further extension of this decentralization over time could involve delegated local control of land tenure and hired labor under contracts, which would enhance the potential incentive effort of this change.

3. Decentralization and incentives in industry; conservation of resources and improved quality.
   - The modernization projects could be the yardsticks for and the recipients of new powers. In these plants, conservation may be attained by use of administrative controls, rationing, and bonuses.
   - Quality criteria could be developed through the emulation of con-

servation and quality standards of East European plants (namely East German), maintained through direct enterprise connections.[12] Later, these model plants may adopt the world market standards of Western enterprises as the criteria for obtaining bonuses. This would represent an incremental approach that avoids immediate implementation of a price system for assessing quality. A system simulating a free market could come later, but it is apparently not even being debated at present.

Technological-Information Revolution

Possibly referring to this problem, Gorbachev indicated that the Soviet Union could not afford to fall further behind. U.S. Secretary of State George Shultz, noting that science and technology of the future will be tied to access to information, said Soviet-led governments "face an agonizing choice: They can either open their societies to the freedoms necessary for the pursuit of technological advance, or they can risk falling even farther behind the West."[13] A dynamic research and development environment requires scientific communication, a reward-oriented system of innovation, and openness within the Soviet Union and to the West to benefit from and contribute to scientific inquiry.

IMPLICATIONS FOR THE UNITED STATES

Gorbachev's diagnosis of the Soviet Union's economic ills seems realistic and his prescriptions strong—even radical—to bring about needed change. If he follows through and is successful, the country's economic health and his own power will be enhanced. By being more attentive to consumer needs, more efficient and responsive to market forces, and more open in relationships with the world market, the Soviet economy may move closer to some of the economic principles with which we identify. With a more modern, efficient economy, engaged in world affairs, the Soviet Union could be a more challenging adversary, although not necessarily more threatening in military terms.

On the other hand, if Gorbachev's strategy fails or is not enacted—if the Soviets fail to increase growth, reduce waste, conserve resources, produce better quality goods, and utilize imports more effectively—the Soviet Union will be weaker as an economic power and will likely be more unstable. Under these conditions, the relative importance of military capability as an instrument of power might be increased rather than diminished, and the likelihood enhanced of their drawing on military force as the only arrow in their great-power quiver.

NOTES

1. The speeches and proceedings of the 27th Party Congress, including discussion of the Five and Fifteen-Year Plans, were reviewed from *Pravda* (Feb. 25–Mar. 7, 1986), and from the daily reports on the Soviet Union of the U.S. Foreign Broadcast Information Service (FBIS) for the period Feb. 25–Mar. 14, 1986. References hereafter to the Plans and Party Congress speeches can be found in these sources.

2. Roger W. Robinson, Jr., "Soviet cash and Western banks," *The National Interest* (Summer 1986), p. 38.

3. John P. Hardt, and Jean F. Boone. "Oil price behavior: Implications for the Soviet Union; Report of the CRS Workshop, June 26, 1986." Congressional Research Service Report 86-886 S. Library of Congress (September 1986), p. 7.

4. Daniel L. Bond, "Centrally planned economies outlook: CPE energy review," Wharton Econometric Forecasting Associates (April 1986), p. 31.

5. Directorate of Intelligence. Central Intelligence Agency. Handbook of Economic Statistics 1986 [McLean, Va.] 1986, p. 73.

6. See the CPSU Central Committee and USSR Council of Ministers resolution "On further improving the management of the Agro-Industrial Complex," *Pravda* (Nov. 23, 1985), pp. 1–2, and the subsequent decree "On further improving the economic management mechanism in the country's Agro-Industrial Complex," *Pravda* (March 29, 1986), pp. 1–2.

7. A sign observed in a printing plant in Tbilisi, Soviet Georgia, described these penalties for being at work in an inebriated condition.

8. Consultations in Moscow, December 1985.

9. For a discussion of the tax-in-kind in the context of the New Economic Policy (NEP), see E. H. Carr, *The Bolshevik Revolution, 1917–1923*, Vol. 2 (New York: MacMillan, 1952), pp. 280–97.

10. See CPSU Central Committee and USSR Council of Ministers

resolutions "On measures to improve the management of foreign economic ties" and "On measures to improve the management of economic, scientific, and technical cooperation with socialist countries," *Pravda* (Sept. 24, 1986), p. 1.

11. Gorbachev speech in Tselinograd, in *Pravda* (Sept. 8, 1985), p. 1.

12. See CPSU Central Committee and USSR Council of Ministers resolution "On measures for a radical increase in the quality of production," *Pravda* (July 2, 1986), pp. 1–2.

13. Quoted by Bernard Gwertzman, "Shultz says technology may aid in easing of East-West tensions," *New York Times* (March 22, 1986).

6 Social Policy Under Gorbachev
Walter D. Connor

This chapter evaluates the social content of various economic, labor, educational, and other policies embraced by the new Soviet leadership. In the first section, "Consumerism and Constraint," Walter Connor examines the economic backdrop for Gorbachev's social policy and concludes that Soviet consumers will find little that is encouraging in the Kremlin's recent economic proclamations and programs. Under Gorbachev the Soviet economy continues to show a "predominance of constraints over opportunities, of tight spots rather than room for maneuvering." Connor's second section details efforts to promote or effect greater discipline in the Soviet Union, in particular Gorbachev's seemingly vigorous efforts to come to grips with the problem of alcoholism. The author next examines Soviet educational policy, especially reform designed to introduce a new form of "tracking" Soviet students that emphasizes secondary vocational-technical schools. Among the potential social consequences of the school reform propounded by Gorbachev, Connor cites the "hereditization" of the Soviet working class. Connor's fourth and fifth sections on the world of work investigate Gorbachev's policies vis-à-vis labor and enterprises, focusing especially on contradictory impulses toward achievement and security, in particular Gorbachev's apparent willingness to tamper with the job security many workers consider to be their birthright. Connor concludes by considering some popular expectations in the early days of the Gorbachev era, many relating to the privileges long enjoyed by the Soviet elite.

While the Soviet government and party call for improved work effort, Connor notes that they fail to provide the requisite positive incentives for stimulating greater productivity, sobriety, or popular enthusiasm. Gorbachev's calls for change do not necessarily imply liberalization of the Soviet system. Indeed, Connor believes that Gorbachev's policies are basically conservative, intended to strengthen the influence of the Soviet state in the social sector. Although Gorbachev appears to be in control at home, many of his policies have been and will no doubt continue to be controversial "even among the elements of the leadership that he has raised to power." Connor suggests that despite Gorbachev's apparent good health, he runs a much greater risk of losing power than did Leonid Brezhev in the early years of his rule.

In little more than a year since taking office, Mikhail Gorbachev has added a vigorous, comparatively youthful "face" to the Soviet leadership, reshaped the composition of the party Politburo and Secretariat, met Ronald Reagan in a summit that Gorbachev's two short-term predecessors had avoided, and managed (rather well) the 27th CPSU Congress and (less well) the Chernobyl nuclear disaster. Although journalistic and expert commentary has, understandably, tended to concentrate on the "high politics" of this period of transition to a post-Stalin leadership generation, the conclusion of the 27th Party Congress and the adoption of the first new party program since Nikita Khrushchev's visionary document of 1961 raises a broader issue—the emergent policy of the Gorbachev leadership in the *social* arena.

Social policy is a broad and vague term, definable only at the risk of drawing limits too narrow or, at the other extreme, of including everything that a strong state may do that has any impact at the grassroots level. Focusing somewhere in the middle of these extremes, this article will first explore some aspects of economic policy as they affect the consumption aspirations and possibilities of the Soviet "man in the street," then examine some themes and policies in the areas of social discipline,

"Social Policy Under Gorbachev," by Walter Connor—revised reprint, included here with permission from PROBLEMS OF COMMUNISM, July–August 1986.

education reform, and work tenure and organization, and finally, touch on the issue of equity and "social justice" in Gorbachev's USSR. It is surely too early to assume that rhetoric and enunciated policy are a clear guide to future Soviet developments, but not too early to explore some possible contingencies arising from the confrontation of new policies and a Soviet population that has become unaccustomed—through the long Brezhnev era and an extended transition to the age of Gorbachev—to bold departures.

CONSUMERISM AND CONSTRAINT

Soviet consumers will find little of great encouragement in the public communications emanating from the Kremlin since the autumn of 1985. Indeed, there are some clearly discouraging indications. The lengthy "Consumer Goods and Services Program" published on October 9, 1985, set goals for the period to 1990—that of the 12th Five-Year Plan—and to the year 2000, the current end-point of so many Gorbachev projections.[1] Near-term goals, if not revolutionary in their promise, seem beyond the reach of the modest-to-minimal growth record of recent years. The program promised to increase production of nonfood commodities by 30 percent above 1985 levels by the year 1990, and 80 to 90 percent by 2000, to achieve better siting of retail outlets, and to arrange for more convenient store hours. Beyond predictable references to clothing and footwear, furniture and refrigerators, the document revealed the continuing "overload" on a central planning apparatus that apparently found it necessary to refer to the production of new types of automatic potato peelers, to promise a 100 percent increase in the production of quartz wristwatches by 1990, and to raise production of videocassette recorders to 60,000 a year by 1990 and 120,000 by 2000.

The program predicted that "payments and benefits provided to the population from public consumption funds will receive further development," but it also set the goal of creating "an extensive and efficiently operating system" of *paid* services, the volume of which is to rise 30–40 percent by 1990 and 110–130 percent by 2000. The commitment to an expansion of paid services was accompanied by comments on improving the quality of services to urban and rural populations and on making services available to all population groups and to people "with different income levels."[2] But if, as seems likely, wage policies will aim at increasing the role of personal income (as opposed to public consumption provisions) in satisfying needs beyond the minimal/normal,[3] the commitment to increasing the proportion of paid services seems likely to benefit mainly higher-income strata.

Moreover, the economy may fall short of fulfilling these promises. There is a perplexing lack of correspondence between the targeted 1986–1990 investment in the "nonproductive" sector and the promised "delivery" from this sector, suggesting that consumption is likely to be an "orphan" in the second half of the present decade. Investment looms large in the targets of the 12th Five-Year Plan, including investment in the energy and agriculture sectors—indeed, Gorbachev has apparently already had to compromise on his public position of mid-1985, which foresaw no significant rises in investment for these sectors.[4] Total investment is targeted to increase by 18–21 percent over the 1986–1990 period, but productive investment is to grow by fully 25 percent.[5] The adverse implication of this for investment in "nonproductive" sectors (health, education, housing, culture), which normally only accounts for about one-quarter of all investment anyway, is clear. This is not a "social budget."

Nor do resources seem to be moving toward the production of mass consumer goods in sufficient numbers to reduce the bottlenecks and pressures that have produced a spectacularly bribe-ridden Soviet economy. Both the Gorbachev rhetoric emphasizing technological investment in leading sectors of the economy (notably machine building) and the discrepancy between the overall investment growth target of some 20 percent and promises of growth in nonfood commodity production of 30 percent by 1990 would seem to tip the scales against any emerging abundance of consumer durables.

That objective circumstances do not favor the Soviet consumer over the next 5 to 10 years, then, seems obvious. This raises for Gorbachev the necessity of mobilizing energies, while disciplining expectations—of brandishing the stick, or its functional equivalent, in the absence of a credible and motivating promise of carrots in the near term. The prospective belt tightening is not simply a matter of policy choice in a slow-growth Soviet economy.[6] For various reasons, neither Eastern Europe nor the West is a likely source of the goods whose import might improve the consumer picture.

Eastern Europe is itself economically strapped, and so long as the Soviets understand that social peace there is maintained partially at the price of guaranteeing living standards that, however threadbare, exceed the Soviet norm, they will not be tempted to treat the region as an interim source of goods to buttress Soviet living standards. Beyond social peace, a modicum of consumerism is necessary to keep Eastern European citizens motivated as producers, at a time when Soviet policies on integration within the Council for Mutual Economic Assistance (CMEA) lean harder on East European economies than hitherto. In a paper prepared for the UN Economic Commission on Europe, Soviet economist Oleg Bogomolov predicted that the CMEA market as a whole "will continue to suffer (at least for the next 5–10 years) from an excess of demand (principally from the USSR) for food and consumer goods. There is, however, relatively little potential for expanding exports of such products."[7]

Western sources will doubtless continue to supply an important component of Soviet consumption, making up shortfalls in grain production. But even in this area relating directly to diet, developments look anything but promising. Falling Soviet oil export revenues reduce available hard currency, intensifying the dilemmas of what to import from the West: technology and capital, grain, or consumer goods?

On the agricultural front, it is now clear that the USSR somehow deserves better luck with weather; yet without it, grain shortfalls will be all the worse, and the claims on diminishing energy export revenues all the greater. The yet-to-be clarified agricultural consequences of the Chernobyl nuclear reactor disaster raise further questions about the quantity and utility of output from farming in the generally marginal producing areas near the plant and, more important, in the Ukrainian breadbasket lands to the south and southeast.

At the 27th Party Congress, Prime Minister Nikolai Ryzhkov spoke of pay raises amounting to 25–30 percent for those in material production, plus allocations for raises for many in nonproduction branches, to be financed by "increased production and efficiency" of labor collectives. These, plus increases in public consumption funds, he predicted, would "lead to really appreciable changes in the living conditions and living standards of very broad strata of society" over the period 1986–1990.[8] It is difficult to square this with Bogomolov's commentary regarding prospects for short-term rises in consumption in the CEMA states: "It is not impossible that until the end of the 1980s resources will be insufficient for the achievement of socially perceptible growth in consumption."[9] The inference is clear: while officials of the Central Statistical Administration will doubtless report some quantitative growth in consumption over the 12th Five-Year Plan period, the dimensions of this growth will not be evident to the public. With stagnation in material conditions, Bogomolov's training and leisure options are unlikely to suffice as incentives for sharply improved work effort.

This brief review of the economic background to social policy in the Gorbachev era reveals a predominance of constraints over opportunities, of tight spots rather than room for maneuver. The regime seems ready to live—or make its subjects live—within those constraints. Along the way, the social policy lines that are emerging, while not altogether clear, seem to promise a peculiar amalgam of activist state intervention in certain areas and the possibility of greater autonomy in others, in a balance as likely to frustrate as to please those at whom it is aimed.

DISCIPLINE

The broad Gorbachev policy stresses discipline: work, sobriety, order, and honesty. In this, it reproduces the style of the Andropov interregnum, but not quite the "campaign" quality of the early months of 1983, when hapless Soviet citizens, shopping during working hours, were dragooned from queues and asked to account for their involvement in what was, after all, a mass behavior phenomenon. Although Western commentary at the time tended to perceive enthusiastic mass support for Andropov's attack on the slackness of behavior, the dishonesty, and the corner-cutting that had become epidemic in the latter years of the Brezhnev period, one may doubt whether such feelings went very deep. The Andropov campaign literally aimed at the "man in the street," long starved of goods and convenient hours in which to purchase them. The stick of discipline was felt immediately; the "carrot" of more convenient store hours and better supplies was a matter of future hopes.

Gorbachev, in contrast, in his first year concentrated more on dismissing, retiring, and otherwise separating from ill-discharged functions party and state leaders at all levels. In so doing, he has given Soviet citizens so inclined something to cheer about, as the incompetent, but especially the corrupt (who used elevated positions to enrich themselves), are laid low. While Soviet citizens surely expect no alteration of hierarchical structures to come from this, it cannot be a matter of total indifference to them that many of the highly placed are finally getting a comeuppance.

Less popular, one must assume, is the campaign Gorbachev has made his own: the one against alcohol abuse in the Soviet Union.[10] Barely had Konstantin Chernenko been buried and Gorbachev settled in the general secretary's chair when *Pravda* and *Izvestia* announced that the Politburo had discussed means of "combatting drunkenness and alcoholism,"[11] setting the stage for further rhetoric, if not action. The first followed, with a Central Committee resolution and a Council of Ministers decree in mid-May.[12] Beyond familiar pieties about expanded programs of medical treatment, the encouragement of more "creative" (namely, sober) use of leisure time, and improvement in the quality of anti-alcohol propaganda, the principal measure was a set of restrictive police policies. Alcohol sales were barred to persons under 21; there were to be no sales of wine and vodka before 2:00 p.m. on workdays; and the number of retail outlets was to be reduced.

In contrast to the past, the Gorbachev regime does seem intent on enforcing such restrictions. Muscovites and visitors report the novelty of "dry" lunches in restaurants, and changes in the previously bibulous pattern of Soviet official entertaining, including events on the Moscow diplomatic round. Soviet reports cite a reduction in retail sales outlets (those selling wine and vodka) of 50 percent during 1985 and a fall in sales amounting to 25 percent for the same year.[13] Restrictions on hours of sale—surely aimed at reducing workplace drunkenness—combined with a crackdown on labor-discipline violations in plants, may have had some positive impact. It was claimed, for example, that the rise in industrial production figures in the fourth quarter of 1985 was attributable in part to more "discipline"—part of which must surely be a lessening of drunkenness, absences, accidents, and general slackness, all related to alcohol.[14]

Over the long term, however, there is ample reason to doubt whether a behavior pattern so deeply rooted can be extirpated, especially habits that have put money in the state's pocket via its monopoly on alcohol production (even as they have taken it away in productivity) and have contributed, in some measure, to the relative political quiescence of a population deprived of liberties and consumer goods long common in the West. If the regime continues to mean business, it may cut the production of liquor further, only to see some of its market ceded to the producers of *samagon* (privately brewed alcohol). Illegal distillers, mainly rural, are targeted in Gorbachev's campaign, but their numbers are large and rural law enforcement is notoriously difficult. Finally, without more goods and services to reward greater discipline and productivity, there will be no positive incentives for the Soviet masses to moderate their drinking.

Discipline at the social level ultimately is a matter of motivation—moral as well as self-interested (whether for gain of reward or avoidance of penalty)—to behave within prescribed patterns (the letter of the law, or something close to it). Moral motivation must be strong indeed if the consequences for the individual are more negative in adhering to the rules than in learning to sidestep them. Here, Gorbachev faces a dual burden. Under Brezhnev as never before, negative incentives to obey laws weakened, while positive incentives failed to grow apace with desires for goods and services. Under these circumstances, the views of the Soviet people about such issues of everyday morality drifted far from the prescriptions of the laws.

Interesting evidence of this emerges in a 1982 Soviet study of popular attitudes toward legal norms—based on a study of 2,000 workers in Moscow industrial enterprises.[15] Respondents were asked about their attitudes toward the negative norms declaring certain acts illegal. Nothing about the results should surprise any student of Soviet affairs—or anyone familiar to any degree with the strictures and opportunities of grassroots Soviet life. Worth noting, however, is not only the very weak support for prohibitions of behavior suggesting participation in the "second economy," but also the clarity of the separation between public and private spheres of moral calculation. According to the study, stealing from the workplace is one thing; from an individual's apartment, something else. Bribing a salesperson is "normal"; being short-weighted by the same, reprehensible. If it is Gorbachev's goal to upgrade public morality to the level of private morality, one can only say that at present the resources to do so, ranging from the coercive to the positively motivating, are in less than adequate supply. Changing such public attitudes will require more than a campaign. Attempting at the outset to change them mainly by negative and punitive policies could produce, in lowered morale and more sophisticated patterns of avoidance, the opposite of the regime's objectives.

EDUCATION: "TRACKING"

Educational reform is not a policy innovation of the Gorbachev era proper (it dates back to 1984), but the new general secretary has made it his own. At the 27th Party Congress he stated that "the reform of general education and vocational schools has started. It must be said that the tempo and depth of implementation of the measures envisaged by the reform cannot yet satisfy us."[16] If we are to take Gorbachev's words at face value (and there are reasons for doing so),[17] they signal commitment to a program with profound implications for social mobility, class composition, and interclass relations, and for some redefinition of the broad notion of "social justice."

The critical elements of the reform aim at a threefold problem: an excess of Soviet teenagers electing to complete academic secondary education, most with an eye toward competing for scarce spaces in higher education; a shortage of job-relevant vocational training for those in the 16–17 year age bracket; and a reluctance or "unreadiness" of those completing academic secondary education to enter the working class. All of these problems, of course, have in recent years been seen against the backdrop of an overall shortage of labor. This has added to the perceived urgency of finding some solutions.

The solution chosen involves a new form of "tracking" for school children, emphasizing a new kind of secondary education institution. It promises to involve state authority at an earlier age in education and career planning for children. The reform proposes to increase "by approximately two times" the number of youths who, after completing "incomplete secondary" schooling (now the eighth grade, but when the reform's new age-six school commencement policy is in place, the ninth grade), go to "secondary vocational-technical schools." This institution (*srednoye professional'no-tekhnicheskoye uchilishche*, in Russian; hereafter SPTU) has grown since the late 1960s out of granting to some upgraded vocational-technical schools (PTUs) the right to grant secondary school diplomas. In the past, the PTUs provided education of a narrowly vocational sort, usually lasting from 8–9 months to one-and-a-half years, and producing, by aim, "workers" for the economy, without granting the diploma of a secondary education.

The SPTUs will evidently absorb the majority of 17 year olds, providing a comprehensive education resulting in both vocational training and a secondary education diploma. Although Soviet surveys indicate mixed feelings—indeed a lack of enthusiasm—on the part of parents and children about such an alternative to the academic track most have selected in the past, many will be given no alternative. In a departure from the "spontaneity" that through the whole post-Stalin era has marked educational choice after the eighth year, admission to academic secondary training will become "selective."[18]

What this means, in effect, is that completion of an academic secondary education—the current 9th and 10th, the future 10th and 11th grades—will be a real option for only a minority of Soviet teenagers, as opposed to the majority today. Granted, those who complete academic secondary schooling in the main do not succeed in entering higher educational institutions (VUZy) today, and have not for some time.[19] But until now they have at least been free to remain in that academic track, and to enter the competition for full admission to VUZy; this will now change. It is also clear that graduates of the "basic" PTUs have not to this point been granted the secondary school diplomas, which the new SPTUs—into which all PTUs are slated for conversion—will be in a position to confer. Thus, though SPTU graduates will have the right-by-diploma to apply to VUZy (albeit only after completing an initial work assignment, it seems), their certification is not likely to be treated in the same manner as that of the minority of favored youth who will receive the traditional academic credentials.

Both numbers and social process are of interest here. Excluding the roughly 10 percent of eight-year school graduates who opt for the paraprofessional "specialized secondary education" from ninth year on, and the now very small number who drop out of school after eight years, the bulk of 15 year olds (in 1979–1980, about 52 percent) has, in the recent past, opted mainly for academic secondary education; only 19.6 percent in the same year opted for SPTU; and 17.7 percent for PTU.[20] On the basis of these figures at least, a doubling in the numbers attending SPTUs (including the "merged" PTU) would shift the proportions radically: about 61 percent would be attending the new institution and only 28.6 percent would remain in the "academic" track.[21]

In social terms, the administrative/selection process outlined above promises to introduce forces at the secondary school level that currently show themselves mainly two years later, during the competition for VUZy entrance. Children of better-paid, better-educated professionals are vastly overrepresented in higher education in comparison with the offspring of workers and peasants. Parental value inculcation, discipline, example, cultural/economic resources, and connections clearly all play a role. Is there any doubt that these factors will also operate at age 15 to determine that recruits to the SPTUs will be largely of average-to-disadvantaged backgrounds, and that those who continue in academic education are likely to be children of already successful parents?

Such a development will intensify the process of the hereditization of the Soviet working class, already well advanced, as working-class children are "tracked" into SPTUs, whose aim is to provide skilled workers for the economy. A hereditized working class, however, would have the potential of becoming a more "class conscious" and combative social force, and a greater problem for political management.

This educational reform represents interventionist social policy—the intrusion of the Soviet state and its representatives into a process hitherto left largely alone. More importantly, the rise of the SPTU as the presumably "model" educational institution of the future reemphasizes the state's tendency to treat its human subjects as "raw material"—to direct them where the state has decided they are needed, and to fit them not only with appropriate manual skills, but also—for this is clearly a presumed benefit of the SPTU—with attitudes appropriate for entrance into the working strata, rather than aspirations to enter into the intelligentsia.

THE WORLD OF WORK

For all the costs—political, psychological, economic, and other—that the Soviet state as collective employer and paymaster, as well as pedagogue and policeman, has imposed on its subjects, it has provided rank-and-file workers guarantees against Western-style unemployment and ensured job security in current jobs at the workplace. Indeed, that issues of the quality of Soviet work life have come into sharper focus in recent years in the writings of Soviet economists and sociologists[22] is a mark of a certain industrial maturity, of having solved in the main the basic problems of providing work and sustenance. While not so critical to the ambitious or the large number each year who do change jobs in the USSR, this security has been, for many, an essential component of a welfare package that links regime and society in a social compact of sorts. It is a benefit to be balanced against the boring, monotonous, sometimes arduous, unmechanized jobs in an industrial economy well behind the West in its evolution toward "post-industrial" or "service economy" characteristics.

There are now signs, however, that the Gorbachev regime may take steps that will imperil this fundamental security without either enriching the nature of work or increasing the rewards for it. Should this prove to be the case, the adjustments required of society could be, collectively, quite remarkable. The reasons for this departure are a "labor shortage" reflecting both demographic realities (the low numbers of young entrants into the labor force and large numbers of workers reaching retirement age) and an abysmally low level of per capita labor productivity. The latter also reflects overmanning as enterprise policy and underemployment of this "stockpiled" labor.

Experiments of limited scope to deal with this problem are not new—for example, starting in 1967, the managers of the Shchekino chemical complex were allowed to dismiss redundant labor and reward those who remained with higher wages from a retained part of wage-fund savings. But the rhetoric confronting inefficient labor utilization—and, implicitly, the underlying job security—has escalated to a new level over the last year and a half. Early calls by Gorbachev for harder work and greater efficiency have been accompanied by action, which although not massive, is certainly more than symbolic. In his 27th Party Congress speech Gorbachev cited the dismissal of 12,000 workers of the Belorussian railway system and cuts in industry and construction personnel of Zaprozh'ye *oblast*, and he held out the prospect that new machinery in agricultural industry might save the labor of as many as 12 million workers by 1990.

The merger of five ministries and a state committee into a unified "State Agro-Industrial Committee" in November 1985 signalled, amid much publicity, the release of several thousand bureaucrats from their jobs. Although it was noted that they would receive benefits equal to their old salaries for a maximum of three months while awaiting placement in new positions, there was no indication of an immediate transfer to other work.[23] Transition payments notwithstanding, they were, effectively, "unemployed."

While one can predict or imagine responses ranging all the way from mild concern to cheers that a set of ministerial bureaucracies had released a reported 47 percent of their apparat,[24] an article in *Sovetskaya Kultura* by labor economist Vladimir Kostakov at the beginning of 1986 raised a more alarming specter. If growth targets for labor productivity for the year 2000 were met, he argued, this would allow a reduction of 13–19 million jobs in manufacturing. He predicted that the sharpness of this process would be "significantly moderated" by routine retirements and by the arrival on the labor scene of smaller cohorts to replace larger existing ones. More significantly, Kostakov wrote of a shift of employment to the service sector—long a low-pay, low-status, understaffed part of the economy—as manufacturing "destocked" especially in the area of non- or minimally-mechanized labor. Indeed, he admitted, in the mid-1980s, "imperfections in the service sphere are harming material production most of all."[25]

Although the image of a more modern economy, somewhat along the lines of "post-industrialism" (without using the term), was a benign one in Kostakov's depiction, the transition from industrial to service employment was cast in terms rather different from those that Soviet audiences are accustomed to hearing: "The need to look for a job, something that many people . . . will certainly face, may also be new and unaccustomed for us. After all, we are used to just the opposite—the job looking for the person."[26]

It was, perhaps, the tone of the commentary, rather than the rough demographic projections, that engendered unease. Whatever the case, an interview with TASS later in the same month gave Kostakov the opportunity to deny that unemployment would result from technological progress and enhanced productivity,[27] and a later article by him in *Sovetskaya Kultura* provided a general discussion of economic progress and its conditions that was less pointed than the earlier one.[28]

Whether this follow-up reflects official Soviet concern with domestic uneasiness or with Western press coverage suggesting that Lenin's sixth lineal heir might preside over the reintroduction of joblessness, the problem is a sensitive one. Soviet labor waste does need correction. The service sector, woefully underdeveloped, is short of manpower by any reasonable international standard (though this is clearly not its only problem). At this point, Gorbachev's policy, while aiming to avert alarmist reactions, has offered no guarantees that things will continue as usual for a largely "tenured" labor force.

Otherwise, the onset of the Gorbachev era seems to have brought little new in labor policy. Predictably, the "brigade method" of shop-floor organization was endorsed at the 27th Party Congress, although the reality of its results remains unclear. Although a 1983 report indicated that more than 50 percent of all industrial workers were working under the brigade method,[29] a 1982 article judged that more than 50 percent of the brigades reported were really "paper" constructs.[30]

Of more interest was Gorbachev's reference in his Party Congress address to the "brigade" or "team" system in agriculture. He held out the prospect that contracting might be "widely disseminated at the level of teams, links, and *families.*"[31] This allusion to a possible return to "family farming" within an unspecified set of collective farm limitations was of particular interest in light of China's successful agricultural de-communalization. But, despite publication since the Party Congress of a lengthy decree on agriculture,[32] there has been no major follow-through on this tantalizing Gorbachev gesture toward private enterprise. It is precisely in this area—where desires to unleash people's capacity to work clash with fears of the social and political consequences of growing inequality and individual enrichment—that the tensions in Gorbachev's social policy may emerge most clearly.

ENTERPRISE, EQUITY, AND SOCIAL JUSTICE

What sort of Soviet society does Gorbachev seek to shape? What combination of impulses toward achievement and enrichment, on the one hand, and quality and security, on the other, is seen as an "appropriate" public mood? What role will private enterprise—and all its more-than-marginal social effects—be allowed to play, if any? What distinctions will Gorbachev regime policy draw between "honest" earning of material advantage, and "unjustified" enrichment of individuals, groups, or classes?

The uncertainties here are many, but not so total as to leave us with no clues. It is worth stating at the outset that there seems to be a distinct lack of readiness to countenance a social outcome of the Hungarian sort. This is more than to say that the USSR will not adopt a "modified" New Economic Mechanism (since such was never possible in any real sense); it is to suggest a distaste among Soviet leaders for the liberalized, decentralized, competitive, and self-exploiting style and content of Hungarian life as it has developed since 1968, for the uncertainties of the mix of private/autonomous and public/dirigiste forces in Hungary. Moscow will tolerate it in Hungary, but will seek to avoid such a consequence in its mix of policies for Soviet society.

The real objectives beyond the immediate rhetoric and policy pronouncements are more difficult to discern, but a few things seem clear. First, within the general commitment to maintaining the Soviet welfare state, one can detect a trend toward the shifting of responsibility for certain matters away from the state, and toward the individual. Kostakov's words on workers seeking jobs, rather than vice versa, bear this message, and this he was not forced to retract. Similarly, one of the thrusts of recent discussion on wage policy (within a general context of "anti-levelling") involved viewing wages and salaries as the main way of satisfying needs beyond those provided for in collective consumption—the implication being that more "needs" can be afforded, the more one earns. It is one's responsibility to earn the money.[33]

Second, this responsibility does not herald a new autonomy for the Soviet citizen in society and economy. Thus far, at least, the Gorbachev regime has offered no large range of private enterprise alternatives for those ready to opt out of the state economy. Though this does not close off all possibility of a future opening to marginal privatization, the current state of mind runs in a different direction. A CPSU Politburo session on March 27, 1986, addressed the bugbear of "unearned income," and *Pravda's* report of the meeting indicated that "plans call for the implementation of legal and other measures aimed at eradicating unearned income from illegal operations, theft, bribery, speculation, and unauthorized use of state-owned transport, machines, and equipment for personal profit."[34] Considering the broad range of behavior that the Soviet mind has been inclined to view as "speculation" and the ubiquity of unauthorized use of state-owned automobiles and trucks, this meeting targeted a great deal of everyday behavior.

At the same time, Gorbachev's Party Congress report suggested some ambivalence—or perhaps, balance—on this score. The general secretary called for consideration of progressive inheritance taxes (one way of getting at "unjust enrichment"), but followed this proposal immediately with a defense of those who gain "additional earnings through honest labor." Could the latter comprise private sector activity?

A Central Committee resolution and a decree of the USSR Supreme Soviet's Presidium—both published on May 28, 1986—made this seem unlikely. Although the documents specify that work in "handicrafts" or "individual labor activity" must be of a specially "prohibited" type to be subject to a catalogue of penalties, they fail to indicate what is legal or what is to be encouraged in the area of private initiative.[35] Unauthorized use of state-owned means of transport is made a matter of administrative penalties (and of criminal prosecution for recidivists), but there is no reference to the possibility of using private automobiles to offer services as part-time taxi drivers in off hours—a modest "privatization" suggested by many economists in recent years.[36]

Proscriptions and penalties for violation of laws will only make social (and ultimately, political and economic) sense if the production of goods and sale of spare parts are boosted and the populace's demand for services is satisfied in the briefest possible time—in other words, if the positive commitments of the Central Committee resolution are met.[37] As indicated above, this is not likely. In the meantime, tight enforcement could force a drying up and a driving further underground of elements of the second economy and a rise in the prices patrons must pay, with no improvement in the net quality of life or social morale. Although USSR General Procurator A. Rekunkov suggested in an *Izvestia* interview five days after the new decree that a law on individual labor activity currently being drafted was aimed not at prohibiting but at developing such activity, and that state registration and taxation (to keep charges from rising too high) would encourage such work,[38] one may doubt whether Soviet citizens will see things that way.

Finally, "social justice" remains an aim, an objective to be pursued so that Soviet citizens perceive as equitable the rules according to which opportunity and benefits are allocated. Here, matters are as interesting as they are complex. Equity and "equality" are not the same thing. However, there is a strong egalitarian bent among a significant segment of the Soviet population, and one may assume that the Brezhnev-era wage policy, which saw a "drift" toward minimization of the earning advantages of engineering and technical personnel over manual workers, and continuing advantages of the latter over people in rank-and-file positions in medicine, education and culture, and other services,[39] responded in some fashion to this bent. Gorbachev seems to have something different in mind—a shake-up in favor of those "underpaid" (from the incumbents' point of view) nonmanual and service-sector occupations, which are expected to increase as a percentage of the labor force when manufacturing de-stocks unneeded workers. In the words of Bogomolov,

fundamental changes may be expected in systems of wage rates and in the differentials between pay of particular categories of workers. For example, the Soviet Union . . . intend(s) to raise the salaries of engineers and technicians, scientists, designers, teachers, and medical staff. . . .[40]

This appears to be a clear commitment to rectify the material disadvantage that those holding degrees have experienced in recent decades. The consequences of a shift in the patterns of inequality in the economic sphere may be all the more important if a new flexibility in prices, a concept frequently touched on during the Congress, means higher prices for many items in demand in retail trade, and if—which seems less likely, given construction material shortages and bottlenecks—cooperative housing construction increases markedly, which would allow a modicum of "custom" building and reflect purchasers' differential buying power.

Still, inequalities in result are one thing; inequalities in opportunity, another. For a system that has never identified justice with equality of outcomes, the critical issue may be opportunity. Tatiyana Zaslavskaya, the Novosibirsk sociologist reputed to have Gorbachev's ear, made a strong argument in early 1986 for a concept of social justice embracing "equal opportunity." Her approach is meritocratic, focusing on conditions that will allow people to develop their own, different, abilities: "children born in families with different social positions must have if not equal, then sufficiently similar 'starting conditions' for the development of their abilities."[41]

Yet it is hard to see how the social process of selection in education, now moving downward (under the above-discussed education reform) in the age structure to the decision point at 15 years of age, will advance these objectives. The assumptions that the selection will be clearly meritocratic, that those intellectually most qualified will continue academic education and pursue its broader career prospects and that the rest will be less talented (if, indeed, such talents can be measured in midadolescence) seem rather far-fetched. The Gorbachev program, such as it is, would seem to leave in place, perhaps strengthen, a major mechanism of inequality.

That "justice" demands a linkage between the quality and quantity of work and its reward is a byword to which, one assumes, most Soviet citizens would subscribe. Current policy, as an official put it, aims

to more accurately and, therefore, more fairly calculate and reward the labor input of each worker and collective and create in them a consistent interest in the utilization of reserves and the increase of production efficiency.[42]

However, this merger of fairness and economic efficiency may result in inequity from the shop floor perspective, which stresses the effort expended rather than the economic result of these efforts. Since the size of material incentive funds is, under new conditions, supposed to be tied to the quality of output (positively through bonuses, and negatively through lower wholesale prices), and quality may depend on more than worker effort (namely, on the adequacies or inadequacies of suppliers, managers, or designers), the workers' position is less secure. In the past, security has consisted, inter alia, in failure to apply tough standards to output. If policy breaks with this past practice, workers who benefit will doubtless see this as just, but those left behind will hardly feel the same.

POPULAR EXPECTATIONS

Generally, the climate of expectations built into today's Soviet population by socialization and experience will not make Gorbachev's tasks any easier. To assume that 1985 and the short-term future have combined a leader whose newness and vigor is welcome to the public with a public mood longing, or at least ready, for a house cleaning to sweep away laziness and corruption and to "get Russia moving again" is to miss another dimension. The Soviet public, habituated to its own sort of welfare state, does expect much from its leaders. That their material expectations are not at Western levels is not the point; rather, it is the contradiction between those expectations, on the one hand, and the inability of economy, as well as the refusal of current policy, to meet them, on the other hand, that may present a long-term problem.

Further insight into the web of expectations and criteria of evaluation found in the Soviet citizenry is emerging from the results of the Soviet Interview Project—a large-scale survey research program conducted among nearly 2,800 Soviet emigrés of the 1970s and early 1980s. For a leadership that might for economic reasons contemplate price rises for a broad range of items, presumably including food, it must be sobering to ponder how those still in the USSR may resemble the emigrés who, in James Millar and Elizabeth Clayton's words, "saw little relationship between the low price of subsidized meat in state stores and supply shortages. They seemed to want (below-cost-of-production) prices and a perfectly elastic supply at those prices."[43]

Even more disturbing to a general secretary evidently committed to a tighter link between performance and (unequal) pay—and to what must be relative consumer austerity over the next few years, and yet who seeks to appeal to younger adults presumably tired of the rule of old men—are emigré survey findings that suggest it is precisely the post-Stalin generation, born in 1941–1960, who views the Brezhnev era as the "peak period" of inequality in Soviet history and are especially attuned to economic issues in judging the regime.[44] The perceptions of Soviet economists, indeed the policy premises of the Gorbachev leadership, are much to the contrary. It would be a signal success if Gorbachev could decouple inequality and "illegitimate" privilege, convincing Soviet citizens in their forties and younger that his wage differentiation policies are equitable and are an antidote to Brezhnev-era excesses that—however visible—existed in a realm of wage/salary inequality nowhere near so extreme, as economists measure things, as under Stalin or Khrushchev.

More workplace discipline, less job security—these are remedies difficult to sell while simultaneously trying to maintain or improve morale. Soviet Interview Project findings indicate that shop-front personnel do not see themselves as the beneficiaries of an easy workpace stemming from overmanning. Paul Gregory finds that "workers and employees performing the actual routine tasks of the economy felt that there was less slack than [did] their supervisors."[45] Redundancy and redeployment are hardly likely to be welcome, especially among blue-collar workers, who will be affected if such policies are pressed forward. In the emigré sample, 37 percent of former workers cited security as a major source of job satisfaction (compared to an average of 31.4 percent for the total sample, and only 21.1 percent for professional people).[46] Even if these figures from an emigré sample cannot be taken as infallible indicators of the feelings of the USSR's citizens in the mid-1980s, they are not likely to be so far off the mark as to vitiate their relevance.

The thrust of Gorbachev's policy line is likely to be controversial. This in turn puts a premium on symbolism and the management of impressions about the direction in which the regime is moving. In this respect, privilege at the top elite level may have symbolic, as well as material import. Elite privileges have been as characteristic of the Soviet welfare state as have fixed prices, low rents, and employment security at the grass roots. These arrangements constitute the world of "special" stores, hospitals, and sanatoria, of the "certificate ruble," which is not a ruble but a wholly different form of currency guaranteeing its possessors access to goods unavailable for any amount of regular Soviet currency.

On February 13, 1986, a *Pravda* review of readers' letters on the topic ventilated a virtually never-discussed feature of Soviet life: the bureaucratic distribution and reservation of material privilege that figures in no reported wage/salary/income statistics. For whatever reason, the published comments were pointed, and while most rhetorically held up to condemnation the "party members" and "communists" who live high, in rejection of classical Leninist modesty, and hinted at an element of corruption, one member of the party since 1940 from Kazan' went even further in the course of a comment that otherwise accepted the justification of large differences in material rewards: "The 'enjoyers of special benefits' will hardly give up their privileges—what is needed here is a law and a thoroughgoing purge of the administrative apparatus."[47]

Yet one can assume that the queues will remain and that the ordinary citizen will not rub shoulders in them with the privileged members of various apparats. This was made clear at the 27th Party Congress when Yegor Ligachev directly criticized *Pravda* for going beyond reasonable limits in its discussion of high privilege.[48] The elite that makes, and presides over the execution of, social policy will continue to inhabit a special preserve. The policy itself—judging by the early indications reviewed here—may bring a new discipline to Soviet society; it may create under new conditions of work organization and reward as many highly-motivated winners as disgruntled losers; it may even, by design or by accident, impart a new dynamism in certain areas of Soviet life. But, all things considered, it is a policy committed to conserving, indeed strengthening, the grip of the state on the critical levers of the social process, to maintaining the old dominant relationship of state over society.

Without arguing the dubious proposition that the Soviet system is today in crisis, or will be precipitated into one by Gorbachev's social policies, it can be contended that the General Secretary's line of attack may prove more controversial than it seems, even among elements of the leadership that he has raised to power. Given the depth of the economic and social problems he faces at home, the complex maze of opportunities and risks to be negotiated abroad with a new foreign policy team, and an activism not likely to be welcome in all quarters, it may be that Gorbachev, however healthy, runs much greater risk of losing power and office than, in retrospect, did Brezhnev in his first five years or so at the helm. Despite the precedent of Brezhnev's 18-year reign, I would rate Gorbachev's chances of being in power in the year 2000 as no better than even, and probably less. For now, however, he seems committed to an activist interventionist policy, whose costs he is willing to bear and to impose as well on more than 270 million Soviet citizens.

NOTES

1. *Pravda* and *Izvestia* (Moscow), October 9, 1985, trans. in *Current Digest of the Soviet Press* (hereafter *CDSP*) (Columbus, Ohio, Nov. 6, 1985), pp. 13–30.

2. Ibid.

3. As the Soviet economist Oleg Bogomolov puts it, in an interesting United Nations paper: "while the social guarantees of the receipt of benefits and services from the social consumption funds are also being reinforced, the role of wages in satisfying demands for 'goods' (e.g. housing) that exceed the socially guaranteed standards is increasing in most of the countries [member states of the Council for Mutual Economic Assistance] under consideration." See UN Economic and Social Council, Economic Commission for Europe, "Perspectives on the ECE regions: Centrally-planned economies in the period up to the year 2000" (Nov. 19, 1985); for presentation at the Feb. 17–21, 1986, meeting of Senior Economic Advisors to ECE Governments), mimeo, p. 14.

4. See, e.g., Gorbachev's speech to a June 11, 1985, Central Committee meeting on accelerating scientific and technological progress; reported in *Pravda* (June 12, 1985).

5. See the discussion in Keith Bush, "Ryzhkov's speech to the Twenty-Seventh Party Congress: A tone of sobriety," Radio Free Eu-

rope–Radio Liberty, *Radio Liberty Research* (Munich), RL 109/86 (March 3, 1986), p. 2.

6. As Prime Minister Ryzhkov noted in his speech at the 27th Party Congress, in 1982 (the second year of the 11th Five-Year Plan) "the increase in the population's real income virtually stopped." *Pravda* and *Izvestia* (March 1, 1986), trans. in *CDSP* (April 23, 1986), pp. 2–3.

7. See Bogomolov, op. cit., p. 14.

8. Ibid., p. 17.

9. Ibid., p. 15.

10. For a recent discussion, see David E. Powell, "The Soviet alcohol problem and Gorbachev's 'solution,' " *The Washington Quarterly* (Washington, D.C.); Fall 1985, pp. 5–15.

11. *Pravda* and *Izvestia* (April 5, 1985), p. 1 of both papers.

12. *Pravda* and *Izvestia* (May 17, 1985), p. 1 of both papers.

13. *Pravda* (Jan. 26, 1985).

14. See the discussion of 1985 performance in Keith Bush, "Soviet plan fulfillment in 1985," *Radio Liberty Research*, RL 47/86 (Jan. 27, 1986).

15. See A. S. Grechin, "Experiment in the sociological study of attitudes toward the law," *Sotsiologichekiye issledovaniya* (Moscow), No. 2 (1983), p. 124.

16. See the text of his report in *Pravda*, (Feb. 26, 1986); trans. in *Foreign Broadcast Information Report, Daily Report: Soviet Union* (Washington, D.C.; hereafter FBIS-SOV) (Feb. 26, 1986), p. 22.

17. Personnel appointments to relevant posts seem to indicate this. On Dec. 5, 1985, *Sovetskaya Rossiya* reported the appointment of Viktor Kaznacheyev as Chairman of the State Committee for Vocational-Technical Education of the Russian Republic; his previous post was party second secretary in Stavropol *kray*—Gorbachev's home turf (see *Radio Liberty Research*, RL 4 11/85, Dec. 6, 1985, p. 3). On Jan. 13, 1986, Radio Moscow announced the appointment of Leningrad City party first secretary Anatoliy Dumachev as Chairman of the USSR State Committee on Vocational-Technical Education. See *Radio Liberty Research*, RL 35/86 (Jan. 17, 1986), p. 5.

18. "Basic directions of the reform of general education and vocational schools," in *O reforme obshcheobrazovatel'noy i professional'noy shkoly, sbornik dokumentov i materialov* (The reform of general education and vocational schools: A collection of documents and materials), (Moscow; Politizdat, 1984), p. 42.

19. For a general discussion, see Murray Yanowitch, *Social and Economic Inequality in the Soviet Union* (White Plains, NY; M. E. Sharpe, 1977), pp. 58–59.

20. Figures are calculated from data in Felicity O'Dell, "Vocational education in the USSR," in J. J. Tomiak (ed.), *Soviet Education in the 1980s*, (London; Croom Helm, 1983), pp. 127–28; in F. R. Filippov, *Sotsiologiya obrazovaniya* (The Sociology of Education), (Moscow; Nauka, 1980), Ch. 3; and in I. Bolotin and V. Chizhov, "Labor resources and the system of public education," *Planovoye Khozyaystvo* (Moscow), No. 8 (1982), p. 103.

21. However, in this area, "make haste slowly" may be the operating principle. The target for the autumn of 1985 involved the enrollment of fully 57.6 percent of all eighth-grade graduates into the ninth grade of academic schools—no great decline over previous years. See *Uchitel'skaya Gazeta* (Moscow, Aug. 22, 1985), pp. 1–2.

22. The best recent treatment of this discussion is found in Murray Yanowitch, *Work in the Soviet Union: Attitudes and Issues* (Armonk, NY; M. E. Sharpe, 1985).

23. *Pravda* and *Izvestia* (Nov. 23, 1985), pp. 1–2 of both papers.

24. As reported by the chairman of the new State Agro-Industrial Committee, Vsevolod Murakhovskiy, in *Literaturnaya Gazeta* (Moscow) (Jan. 22, 1986). However, the same source reported that as of late February (about three months after the redundancies were announced), "virtually all" of the 3,200 released had new jobs. See *Sel'skaya Zhizn'* (Moscow) (Feb. 21, 1986).

25. In *Sovetskaya Kultura* (Moscow) (Jan. 4, 1986); trans. in *CDSP* (Feb. 19, 1986), pp. 1–4.

26. Ibid.

27. TASS interview, Jan. 16, 1986 (see *Radio Liberty Research*, RL 35/86, Jan. 17, 1986, p. 11).

28. *Sovetskaya Kultura* (Feb. 1, 1986), p. 3; trans. in *CDSP*, (Feb. 19, 1986), pp. 4–5, 23.

29. N. Safronov, Ya. Shagalov, and A. Shirov, "Reserves for increasing labor productivity in USSR industry," *Sotsialisticheskiy Trud* (Moscow), No. 7 (1983), p. 13.

30. A. A. Gorel'skiy, "Defining brigade economic accounting," *EKO* (Novosibirski), No. 7 (1982), p. 122.

31. *Pravda* (Feb. 26, 1986); emphasis added.

32. *Pravda* and *Izvestia* (Mar. 29, 1986); trans. in *CDSP* (May 7, 1986), pp. 10–15.

33. Bogomolov speaks of "making workers' levels of real consumption more closely dependent on their incomes." "Perspectives on the ECE regions," op. cit.,. p. 14.

34. *Pravda* (Mar. 28, 1986), p. 1.

35. *Pravda* (May 28, 1986), pp. 1–2.

36. See, for example, Abel Aganbegyan in *Trud* (Moscow) (Dec. 12, 1982), p. 2.
37. *Pravda* (May 28, 1986), pp. 1–2.
38. *Izvestia* (June 2, 1986), p. 3.
39. Whether such a pattern will be reversed is another question. The "inertial" drive away from the peak inequalities of the Stalin era is, after all, a matter of nearly three decades of policy and "drift"—a long time. At the 27th Congress, Ryzhkov even noted that "elements of wage-levelling . . . have intensified recently." *Pravda* and *Izvestia* (Mar. 4, 1986), trans. in *CDSP* (Apr. 23, 1986).
40. Bogomolov, "Perspectives on the ECE regions," op. cit., p. 14.
41. See *Sovetskaya Kultura* (Jan. 23, 1986), p. 3.
42. *Izvestia*, (Feb. 8, 1986), p. 3; trans. in *FBIS-SOV* (Feb. 13, 1986), p. 53.
43. James R. Millar and Elizabeth Clayton, *Quality of Life: Subjective Measures of Relative Satisfaction*, Soviet Interview Project (SIP) Working Paper No. 9 (Urbana-Champaign, IL; Feb. 1986), mimeo, p. 10.
44. Donna Bahry, *Politics, Generations and Change in the USSR*, SIP Working Paper No. 20 (Urbana-Champaign, IL: Apr. 1986), pp. 34–36.
45. Paul R. Gregory, *Productivity, Slack and Time Theft in the Soviet Economy: Evidence from the Soviet Interview Project*, SIP Working Paper No. 15 (Urbana-Champaign, IL: Feb. 1986), p. 23.
46. Millar and Clayton, *Quality of Life*, op. cit., Figs. 12A–12D.
47. *Pravda* (Feb. 13, 1986), p. 3; trans. in *CDSP* (Mar. 12, 1986), p. 2.
48. See *Pravda* and *Izvestia* (Feb. 28, 1986); trans. in *CDSP* (Apr. 9, 1986), p. 9.

7 Soviet Culture: New Attitudes Toward the Arts
Irwin Weil

In his chapter on Soviet culture, Irwin Weil provides a brief survey of Russian cultural life from the late nineteenth century to the present. Just as he found cultural vibrancy to exist during the waning days of tsarist despotism, so he maintains that despite Stalin's attempt to obliterate conventional Russian and revolutionary Soviet avant garde culture, and despite the heavy hand of Soviet officialdom since Khrushchev, a repressed though very real cultural vibrancy still exists in the Soviet Union, a vibrancy naturally at odds with most official norms. Weil remarks that in intellectual circles, something is "obviously stirring" in the Soviet Union since Gorbachev's assumption of power. Like many Soviet intellectuals, he would like to think that Gorbachev will loosen the political reins that govern Soviet cultural life, if not give free rein to Soviet writers and artists. Weil devotes several paragraphs to the career of Yevgeny Yevtushenko and his standing in Russian cultural circles. He takes heart in Yevtushenko's recent speech before the Russian Branch of the Soviet Writers' Union in Moscow, in which he criticized many of the shortcomings of Soviet society. At the same time, however, Weil notes the fate of Yuri Lyubimov, the former director of the Taganka Theater in Moscow, who overstepped the bounds of political propriety and suffered the consequences.

Of all the long-term problems facing Soviet society, few have been more enervating than that of alcoholism. Anyone familiar with Russian history knows that alcoholism has been a fairly serious problem for centuries. The draconian campaign instituted tuted by Mikhail Gorbachev against drinking only demonstrates the extent of the current problem. The following joke circulated in Moscow some years back:

When [then-Vice President] Richard Nixon visited the Soviet Union [in 1959], he was impressed by nearly everything he saw, but he told First Secretary Khrushchev that he was especially impressed by the number of drunks he saw in the streets. Khrushchev, deeply offended, countered, "That's nonsense. We have no drunks in the Soviet Union. Here is a rifle. You may shoot anyone you see who is drunk." Nixon had a field day; he shot people right and left all day long. When Khrushchev subsequently visited Washington, he asked Nixon to return the favor. Nixon was hesitant at first, saying that "that sort of thing is not normally done in this country." In the end, however, he relented, reasoning that "reciprocity is reciprocity." He handed Khrushchev a rifle and said, "All right, you can shoot anybody you see drunk." Khrushchev stalked the streets of Washington for hours without success. Finally he saw a man staggering badly, so he let him have it. The man fell immediately, and the triumphant Khrushchev felt much better. The next day this headline was read in the American press: "Police investigating mysterious murder of Soviet Ambassador."

This story tells us something about the magnitude of the alcohol problem in the Soviet Union, but it also tells us something about the self-deprecating nature of Soviet humor. There are literally thousands, perhaps tens of thousands, of stories that real masters know by heart. All of these anecdotes represent the myriad ways in which the Soviet people, especially the Great Russians, poke fun at themselves. They have a particularly strong and acidulous way of undermining many officially proclaimed attitudes.

As people inside and outside the Soviet Union have watched Gorbachev trying to deal with such issues as alcoholism with a mixture of exhortation and legislation to change the offending behavior, they have similarly viewed him attempting to change and reanimate the sluggish Soviet economy. Of course, many of his proposed reforms and changes arouse the strong opposition of bureaucrats and administrators who have long profited from the system that spawned the weak economy in the first place.

One must understand that Soviets, not just Americans or other outsiders, are very critical of their own economy. This is not something new in Soviet history. For generations politicians have been coming to power and arguing inside the Party about how they were going to transform an economically weak country into an economic giant. The original Bolsheviks believed they had most of the answers. Then they gave way to another generation, and the arguments started all over again. One of the great slogans of the Bolshevik Revolution promised that the new order would turn Russia upside down and make her into a modern country. As a matter of fact, Lenin once said, "We are going to weld the Russian soul onto the American worker who rolls up his sleeves and gets to work." When Khrushchev visited New York in 1959, one of the first things he did was have himself photographed with his sleeves rolled up. He told curious reporters simply, "I want to be like an American." Obviously, old Leninist dictums die hard, even when they flatter America. Thus, the Bolsheviks were determined to make the Russian people more like Americans, people who supposedly really knew how to work. Despite subsequent developments, this remained an attractive idea to later Soviet rulers.

As Dimitri Simes has noted in Chapter 4, most of the revolutionaries surrounding Lenin were internationalists, intellectuals who had read widely and written for an international audience. They were aware of what was going on in the world, unlike the relatively provincial Soviet leaders we have become accustomed to since Stalin's time. These leaders were bent on modernizing a society and an economy that everyone regarded as weak and backward, constituting the real "sick man of Europe." Of course this term is applied historically to the Ottoman Empire, but the Bolsheviks viewed the Russian Empire in the same light.

Lenin and those close to him were at least partially representative of the old Russian intellectuals, although Lenin and Trotsky often cursed the intelligentsia. Most were sensitive to all kinds of literature, indeed, to all kinds of culture. They believed that their ideology would produce an entirely new species of human being. Some of the portraits of these Bolshevik intellectuals in the Lenin Museum near Red Square in Moscow were rubbed out during the Stalin era. When the intellectuals were purged during the Terror, they ceased to exist historically, too. Photographs and paintings of men such as Trotsky, Bukharin, and Zinoviev were destroyed or altered. In one painting of Stalin speaking at Red Square, it is obvious that some of the faces do not quite fit in with the others. Stalin's artists were not skillful as they might have been in replacing original faces with new ones.

The same can be said of Soviet culture in general, namely, that Soviet society cannot quite make its values fit neatly with either the old, inherited ways of imperial Russia, the early days of the Bolshevik regime, or the high aspirations set forth for the new way of dealing with contemporary reality.

As was previously noted, Lenin and his closest associates belonged to the Russian intelligentsia, many members of which considered Russia to be a very sick country, especially in social and economic terms. But can pre-revolutionary Russia be considered culturally poor? The names of Dostoyevski and Pushkin, among others, would indicate otherwise. These literary giants were two of the most energetic examiners of the human soul who ever lived. Similarly, we should consider accomplishments in Russian dance, especially ballet, in music, and in other fields of art as well.

Pre-revolutionary Russia was very rich in terms of culture and in artistic efforts to understand the nature of the human soul. Many have argued, some recently, that Russian creativity came to an abrupt end with the Revolution, but this contention flies in the face of historical evidence. At the time of the Revolution and immediately after, there were very powerful movements in all the arts. Many of the trends we tend to think of as French, Italian, German, or American from the 1920s to the 1940s and beyond either started in Russia or received powerful creative impulses there. French impressionism, for example, owes much to the Russian artists who worked during the first three decades of this century. The names of Kandinsky, Malevich, Lisitsky, Rodchenko, and Popova are representative of a number of great artists who were experimenting with all kinds of interesting new forms at the time of the Revolution. The same period saw experimentation in music, architecture, poetry, and other literary forms. A virtual explosion of ideas took place in the fields of costume and dress design.

Many of these innovative artists were enthusiastic communists who believed that Lenin was a kind of modern god come down to earth to show them a new and better way. They believed that communism would produce a new kind of human being, a supposition that led to various excesses like the so-called *proletkult*, the idea of proletarian culture producing a new culture entirely independent of the old one. In Mayakovsky's words, the new culture would take the Shakespeares, Cervanteses, and Tolstoys of the world and throw them over the side of the ship of history in order to create an entirely different kind of art. Unfortunately for many of the artists and intellectuals who held similar views, the kind of art that developed in the Soviet Union was not what they had envisioned, and the very communist government they had enthusiastically embraced turned around and squashed them. By the end of the 1920s, the so-called avant garde had been virtually destroyed. Today we owe much of our knowledge of the Soviet avant garde to a very courageous man, George Costakis, a Greek born in the Soviet Union, who had worked for the Canadian embassy and, taking advantage of a certain kind of protection, saved hundreds, indeed thousands, of magnificent art works from officially sponsored destruction.

What emerged in place of the avant garde was a very conservative apparatus that wanted to see art conform to the political imperatives of the Soviet regime and support the building of a new industrial economy and society. Eventually the so-called five-year-plan literature appeared, which changed the old Hollywood formula to something like this: boy sees tractor, boy falls in love with tractor, boy marries tractor. By the time of Stalin's death, "socialist realism," this attempt to put everything into an ideological straight jacket, had become so perversely strong that it had become extremely difficult for artists to produce work that was really alive.

During Stalin's rule, many of the very best Soviet artists, writers, and intellectuals suffered in miserable silence or went to their deaths because they could not conform in a fashion acceptable to the regime. If anything, Stalin's domestic terror exceeded Hitler's. In just a few years Hitler and his henchmen destroyed German culture, in particular the once great German universities such as Heidelberg, Leipzig, Göttingen, etc. To this day German universities have not regained the relative position they once held in European culture. The destruction of German culture was the result of twelve years of totalitarian rule, which, of course, was particularly murderous for anyone who was Jewish in Germany. But if one was not Jewish and agreed to keep one's mouth shut, by and large one was left alone by the Nazis.

In contrast, Stalin exercised power for over twenty-five years. Whether or not one kept one's mouth shut made little difference in Stalin's Russia. One was eliminated equally. By the time of Stalin's death, his regime had managed to murder over 80 percent of the "old Bolshevik" leadership, the people who had made the Bolshevik Revolution. The dead included the flower of what had once been the Soviet intelligentsia. Stalin had been determined to liquidate them and their influence. In this he had the support of certain segments of the Soviet population that thought they had reason to be angry with the intelligentsia. Thus, the murderousness of the Stalin regime was in part a reflection of the hostility of broad masses of the Soviet population toward the intellectuals whom they held responsible for many of their miseries. But despite Stalinist oppression and terror, despite the crude and brutal attempts to rub out, often quite literally, the art of the past, the earlier traditions of Russian and early Soviet culture managed to survive.

The first post-Stalinist generation of the mid-1950s and 1960s struggled against the officially sanctioned Socialist Realism of Stalin's time and looked for inspiration to the earlier traditions of Russian culture. A case in point is that of Boris Pasternak, the writer who died in the early 1960s after absorbing a terrible Soviet government attack for his novel, *Dr. Zhivago*. The location of Pasternak's grave has never been officially announced in the Soviet press, but one can visit it in Peredelkino, the writer's colony outside Moscow. The grave never lacks attention; there are always flowers. As a matter of fact, there are also usually potatoes on the grave. Potatoes are an old Slavic symbol of resurrection, and for many young people, Pasternak, through the power of his poetry, represents the resurrection of Russian culture. (In February 1987 it was announced by the Soviet Press that *Dr. Zhivago* would be published, and a few weeks later Pasternak was posthumously reinstated in the Soviet Writer's Union—editors' note.)

At the time of President Kennedy's assassination in 1963, I received three letters from Soviet friends. One was written by a 27-year-old graduate student. The fact that he was 27 years old meant that he had been born after the publication of the last edition of Josip Mandelshtam's poetry. In order to write a letter of consolation for the grief he felt at the loss of President Kennedy, who was very popular with young people in the Soviet Union, he quoted a line from one of Mandelshtam's most famous short poems:

Chelovék umiráet—pesók ustyvaet sogretyi, I vcheráshnee sólntse na chérnykh nosílkakh necút.
[A man dies. The heated up sand cools down, and yesterday's sun is carried out on a black stretcher.]

The succession of stresses and the placement of consonants in the Russian transliteration indicate why Mandelshtam is almost universally considered, even by today's official Soviet spokesmen, one of the greatest masters of the powerful Russian language in the twentieth century. Mandelshtam represents the older Soviet tradition, but this was the tradition that spoke to the younger generation in the Soviet Union after Stalin's death. It still speaks to the younger generation in the Soviet Union today.

In cultural (and to a certain extent political) terms, the period in Soviet history from the death of Stalin until the early 1960s is commonly referred to as "the thaw." The term came from the title of Ilya Ehrenburg's controversial novel, *The Thaw* (1953). Just as the novel's title referred to the spring thawing of a stream that had long been frozen, it was hoped that a new, political season with warm breezes would cause a long-frozen cultural life to flow again. Indeed, as a result of the cultural thaw, many young writers came into bloom, among them Yevgeny Yevtushenko.

It is instructive to look at Yevtushenko's career, because its twists and turns reflect the tortuous road taken by many intellectuals after Stalin's death. I first learned about Yevtushenko in 1960, when he was in his early twenties. I walked into a bookstore and started talking with a young female clerk, who, like many people who work in literary bookstores, was articulate and lively—not the sort of clerk one usually confronts at Soviet service counters. When I indicated I was very interested in Russian literature, especially poetry, she glanced left and right to make sure nobody was looking and extracted a book from under the counter with unbelievable speed. I asked what it was. She countered, "You'll see." I asked who the author was. She again replied, "You'll see." When I read the book that night in the privacy of my hotel room, I discovered that the author was Yevgeny Yevtushenko.

I do not consider Yevtushenko to be a Pushkin or a Shakespeare, but it was clear that his was a fresh voice. Here was somebody who obviously knew something about the rhythms of the Russian language, somebody who did not simply kowtow to the deadly official line in poetry. He obviously had been influenced by Mayakovsky, but was trying to go beyond him. For many reasons I found his writing very interesting. When I returned to the bookstore the following day, the same clerk explained that Yevtushenko appealed to many of the younger people in the Soviet Union. His appearance on the literary scene had aroused a great deal of enthusiasm.

Yevtushenko soon was involved in many sensational activities. He went abroad and made some critical comments that Soviet officials did not want to hear. They called him back and censured him. Apparently he did not learn his lesson well, because he proceeded to write some poems that really antagonized the powers-that-be when he wrote about the punishment battalions that had existed during the Second World War.

Perhaps his most famous poem was "Babii Yar," which touched the question of anti-Semitism in the Soviet Union. Babii Yar was a place outside Kiev where 60,000 Jews had been murdered by the Nazis. It was made up of numerous ravines, which were very convenient for SS executioners. Jews were marched to the upper edges of the ravines where they were shot, their bodies falling into adjacent hollows, where they were buried. One of the most horrible aspects of what happened at Babii Yar was that not all the victims were dead when they were buried. Witnesses told me that for days afterwards they could see the ground heaving. For years after the war, the Soviets steadfastly, and inexplicably, refused to put up a monument at Babii Yar. When they eventually did so, it read: "Here at this place 100,000 citizens of the Ukraine were killed by the Nazi usurpers." There was not a word about the fact that most of the victims had been Jews. For many people this symbolized the callous official Soviet attitude toward the Jewish victims of Nazism that developed after the war. Yevtushenko's poem, which attacked anti-Semitism by using Babii Yar as its horrible symbol, proved as moving to Soviet intellectuals as it was irritating to the Soviet government.

In the ensuing years, however, it seemed that Yevtushenko had curbed his rebellious tendencies. In the 1970s certain critics in the West and the Soviet Union grew increasingly suspicious of him, some accusing him of serving as the regime's stooge. One common denigration was that he was not serious, that he "played with dolls" [On igraet v kukly]. I was always reluctant to accept such criticism. I held that it was very easy for Western critics to condemn Yevtushenko for not being sufficiently courageous. They weren't living in the Soviet Union. They didn't have to walk a political tightrope. On the other hand, Soviet critics of Yevtushenko among the intelligentsia might well have earned some right to criticize him. One must understand that Soviet literature is read by millions of people. One of the great things about the Soviet Union is the breadth and depth of people who like to read or are actively engaged in cultural life. In the USSR, cultural life is not considered a luxury or simply entertainment and diversion as it often is in America. When Soviet artists speak, even in a whisper, people listen closely, and the sound reverberates. A whisper there is sometimes stronger than a roar here.

Soviet cultural life is at the center of public feeling and imagination. Hence, it is all the more interesting to observe recent developments on the cultural scene, in particular Yevtushenko's activities. When Gorbachev came to power, the Soviet intellectuals, the Soviet reading and listening public, had been through many turns of the screw. As many Soviets put it: "The accordian goes out; the accordian goes in. We know that one generation is more liberal; another is more conservative. As soon as we stick our necks out, we are going to get into trouble."

In the 1960s many intellectuals and artists tried to secure more creative freedom for themselves by taking one tiny step after another. They did not challenge the party; indeed, they sought to win the confidence of the party in the hope that more freedom would be given to them. The invasion of Czechoslovakia in 1968 taught them what they already knew: that the party would act with strong repression whenever it felt challenged. They had seen the avant garde movement of the heady 1920s brutally crushed. They had experienced "the thaw." They had participated in the partial resurrection of the avant garde tradition. They also knew that whatever the government might say at any particular moment had to be taken with a great dose of skepticism. And so it is today with the intellectuals and artists under Gorbachev.

The Taganka Theater in Moscow mirrors the environment in which Soviet intellectuals live. For years the Taganka was a marvelously live theater directed by Yuri Lyubimov, who put on daring stage productions of plays by Shakespeare, Molière and other classic writers, the content of whose plays is mirrored in Soviet history. Macbeth, of course, is a bloody murderer who presumably existed in Scotland long ago. But when Soviet citizens see *Macbeth*, they do not think of Scotland. They think instead of their own country and certain kinds of murders that took place there not so long ago. When they see the character of Hamlet struggling with the king, they instinctively interpret it in terms of their own lives.

Lyubimov put on many plays with daring kinds of productions. He also staged a production of Bulgakov's famous novel, *The Master and Magarita*, which everyone in Moscow wants to see. For many years it played once a month at the Taganka

Theater. Bulgakov wrote this book as a combination of the rewriting of the New Testament, a rewriting of the Faust tale, and a satire of Soviet life, all put into one novel. *The Master and Magarita* was never published in Bulgakov's lifetime (he died in 1940); it would have cost him his head in Stalinist Russia. But it was published in the 1960s in bowdlerized form; subsequently, the complete manuscript was sent abroad so the book could be published in toto. It became quite a sensation and a controversial topic in the Soviet Union.

In Moscow people clammered to see Lyubimov's stirring theatrical performance of the novel. Huge crowds milled outside the theater hoping to squeeze inside. At the end of the play, actors marched around a series of poster-size photos of Bulgakov. The audience's effusive applause, as well as Lyubimov's production, constituted a moving and long-overdue tribute to Bulgakov's memory and genius.

About three years ago Lyubimov travelled to England. In an interview with the London *Times* he said that "the Communist Party has two wings, and I hope they use both of them to fly straight to hell." Lyubimov's days were numbered. About a month after the article appeared, he was stripped of his Soviet citizenship, and he is now staging plays and operas in the West. This is very sad, for the Taganka Theater had been a tremendously live presence in Moscow, very different from the Moscow Art Theater, which by now has become a kind of musty museum of Stanislavsky's ideas—in their own time equally revolutionary, but by now settled into a predictable routine. (Early in 1987 Lyubimov was approached by a Soviet official in Washington, D.C., concerning the possibility of returning to Moscow. Whether Lyubimov would return even if a formal invitation were offered was not clear—editors' note).

In assessing the various attempts of Mikhail Gorbachev to change Soviet reality, one must keep in mind the vibrancy of Soviet cultural life. When a new Soviet leader begins talking about changing industry, getting the country moving again, and the like, many Soviet citizens are interested in a corollary question: "What is he going to do for, or to, art and literature?" My Soviet friends inform me that Gorbachev has replied to this question by saying, "Look, we have to deal with first things first. I don't know anything about literature"—a refreshing admission from a Soviet leader. He continued by saying the government will have to deal with the first priorities first, but that after the February Congress, there would be some changes in literature as well. My Soviet friends seem to believe that change is indeed in the offing. The question is: what kind?

One possible answer lies in the recent words and deeds of Yevgeny Yevtushenko, the one-time *enfant terrible* of Soviet letters. In December 1985 Serge Schmemann, the Moscow correspondent for the *New York Times* and a man of Russian background who knows the Russian language and, from all accounts, Soviet culture and society very well, reported that Yevtushenko had recently made a speech at the Russian Branch of the Soviet Writers' Union in Moscow. According to Schmemann, Yevtushenko had criticized many of the ways things had been done before and the fact that Soviet writers have turned their eyes from real problems, that they have refused to deal with the terrible deaths and murders that had taken place under Stalin, just as they have refused to deal with many terrible things that have happened to and in their country since Stalin's time. He said, "Yes, it is a wonderful thing to criticize what the Americans do in Central and South America, but what right have you to criticize things there if you cannot criticize things in Omsk, and in Riazan, and in Moscow as well?" These were bold words for somebody speaking in Moscow, but he did not stop there. "Furthermore," he said, "it is a disgrace that we have such things as controlled stores in this country to which only a few people have access. You know that everyone at this congress has special coupons in his pockets to go to stores that the average Soviet citizen may not enter to get special goods. I have them in my pocket just as you have them in yours. There shouldn't be this institution in a socialist country."

In his speech Yevtushenko attacked one thing after another that was sacred to the Soviet regime. Interestingly, parts of his speech, along with several other addresses, were published in *Literaturnaya Gazeta*, probably the most serious of all the Soviet literary publications. The next day the *New York Times* published the full text of Yevtushenko's speech. Those parts that had been excised by the *Literaturnaya Gazeta* appeared in italics. No doubt somebody in Moscow is furious. This incident demonstrates the difference between the kinds of things that can be said and the kinds of things that can be printed in Gorbachev's Moscow at this stage of the general secretary's career. It is interesting to note that Yevtushenko was not the only one talking this way, although it was only Yevtushenko who had the courage, or sufficient protection in the Soviet regime, to give the text of his speech to a foreign correspondent.

In all likelihood, Yevtushenko did not act on his own initiative. I am quite sure that he spoke out only because he knew his group had protection somewhere in the Communist Party. The interesting question is, where in the party? A natural conclusion, which may be based on wishful thinking, is to say that it came from Gorbachev or somebody close to him. Maybe the writers were simply "raising their sails," the metaphor the *New York Times* used, to see which way the wind was blowing, hoping it was blowing in the direction they wanted to go. On the other hand, maybe their speeches were cleared in advance by the government, which said in effect, "Look, you go ahead, and let's see what happens." In any case, it looks as if there is at least the possibility of a certain kind of positive change under Gorbachev along with the realization that if Soviet literature is ever again to have any kind of authority in its open, published form, it must be able to compete with *samizdat*, the Soviet underground literature. In this regard, it was rather amusing to read in the *New York Times* some time ago that *Pravda* had accused *Izvestia* of being dull. That certainly was a case of the pot calling the kettle black. Still, it indicates a new kind of openness.

In the very recent past, we have the example of the sad events at the Chernobyl atomic reactor site. In connection with the resulting international furor, it is instructive to remember another part of Yevtushenko's December 1985 speech. He contrasted two events: the terrible Mexico City earthquake, which received enormously detailed coverage in the Soviet press, and aroused national sympathy for the Mexican victims; and the terrible Tashkent earthquake, which received very sparse coverage in the same Soviet press. Yevtushenko asked a poignant rhetorical question: "Are we Soviets less worthy of support than the Mexicans?"

Immediately after the Chernobyl disaster, the world was ready to pose the same question: how openly would the Soviets deal with this tragedy for its citizens? The initial reaction was less than encouraging. During the first two weeks after the Swedish report had initially informed the world of a greatly increased level of radioactivity in the atmosphere, the Soviets went into their classically defensive stance: cover-up blanketed their responses. To be sure, the Western press, exhibiting more concern for the effect of the disaster on the commodities market than on human beings, did little to encourage openness on the part of the Soviets. But that did not excuse a cover-up of such a universally important matter.

After the first two weeks, however, the nature of the Soviet announcements began to change. Errors were admitted, information began to be released, and it looked as if a much more open policy had been adopted. This was very much in line with the pronouncements of the 27th Party Congress in February. Although the Party spokesmen did not respond as Yevtushenko's earlier remarks make us think he would have liked them to, there was still a reiteration of Gorbachev's determination to bring about a more thoughtful and open policy concerning information and literature.

Something is obviously stirring in the Soviet Union. At a minimum it is simply the widely held notion that large numbers of readers would like to see a different kind of literature and press. It goes without saying that the real writers and intellectuals feel this way, as well as the genuinely educated people. Perhaps even large segments of the general population feel this way, too. It seems safe to say that there obviously are people within the party and government who feel this way, officials who recognize that Soviet literature in its official form is dull and is taken no more seriously by an intelligent reader than the Soviet press is. In fact, many Soviet leaders do not read their own press for real information; they turn instead to a Russian language version of the Western press, which, of course, they do not release to the general population.

If this movement toward more openness continues and if the government feels itself strong enough to allow it to gain a certain level of maturity, what a wonderful future there could be for Soviet literature, Soviet artists, and the Soviet public. Millions of Soviet citizens can only hope that the government will follow through on some of the promises apparently made by Gorbachev and his associates concerning cultural matters.

In conclusion, I would hope that people in the United States would make it clear through our unofficial sources and, if possible, through our government ones, that we sympathize with our true Soviet friends. Just as Americans look back to their traditions of tolerance, openness, and freedom of speech, Soviets look back to the very best parts of the Russian tradition, which Pasternak embodied so well in his time. Let us affirm that we would like these two great traditions to come together in a world that could be a lot better than the one we live in now. I can only hope that our Soviet friends, and there are millions of them, may find their way to this kind of resolution. And I hope that we in this country do our very best to show them that we will greet them with open arms and sympathetic hearts, and that we are on their side in their efforts to live the best life they can. If they can achieve this, it will benefit us and the entire world.

8 Gorbachev and the 27th Party Congress of the CPSU

J. Martin Ryle

In the concluding chapter, J. Martin Ryle focuses on Mikhail Gorbachev's major speech to the 27th Party Congress. In so doing he touches upon many, if not most, of the themes and topics explored in the first seven chapters, including alcoholism, summitry, and the prospects for economic and political reform in the Soviet system. After briefly surveying the political and economic legacies that Gorbachev has inherited, especially the Stalinist one, Ryle enumerates various ways in which the words of Gorbachev and his closest associates at the Party Congress would seem to indicate that change is in the offing. In his "political report" Gorbachev was at least more forthright than some of his predecessors in pointing out certain deficiences in the Soviet system and assessing various dilemmas facing policymakers. Yet, as Ryle points out, the voices of the old guard were heard as well. The words and manner of Mikhail Gorbachev impressed some of our authors, but for others actions speak louder than words. Ryle suggests that if Gorbachev is to be successful in implementing reforms, he must enlist the enthusiastic support of the state bureaucracy and party apparatus as well as of the working public. Inspiring the public to fulfill its responsibilities will be difficult unless the officials accept the reductions in power and perquisites that meaningful reforms anticipate.

INTRODUCTION

Mikhail Gorbachev could hardly have orchestrated more ideally his first year at the helm of the Soviet state. His accession to power upon the death of Konstantin Chernenko in March 1985 was followed by a rapid imposition of the new leader's priorities and personality upon his country. He attacked laxity in the factories, reiterating a theme first struck by Andropov; he launched a crusade against drunkenness; he reinvigorated the "peace offensive," especially in Europe; he oversaw the publication of a revised program of the CPSU; he met with Ronald Reagan in Geneva; he demoted several rivals. Crowning this whirlwind of activity, the 27th Congress of the CPSU provided the new general secretary a fine opportunity to criticize his predecessors, cajole and inspire his contemporaries, and prescribe the medicine required to bring the ailing system back to health.

It has become a commonplace that Gorbachev faces severe economic, demographic, social, and international problems. In its almost seventy years, the Soviet Union has earned worldwide respect, not only for its military prowess, but also for its economic growth, social stability, and spectacular technological achievements. But no state can rest upon accomplishments long past, and the recent Soviet record contains little beyond space exploits and military strength to reinforce that hard-won respect. Embroiled in the ill-advised Afghan war, facing a steady erosion in economic growth rates, and suffering from extraordinarily poor labor productivity, the Soviets in the post-Brezhnev era must either accept declining influence in the world arena or steel themselves to extensive reforms, even at the risk of unpredictable and potentially destabilizing side effects.

Several prominent Western scholars, including Marshall Goldman and Seweryn Bialer, observed during 1985 that the measure of Gorbachev's determination for reform and his political skill in achieving change would be visible in the revised party program, published in October, and the 27th Party Congress, February 24–March 8, 1986. These same scholars have since expressed disappointment that the projected reforms appear superficial, leaving unaltered the structure of Soviet economic and social institutions that have failed in the past to respond adequately to steadily deepening crises.[1] Gorbachev has certainly proposed nothing that would directly challenge either the party or the bureaucracy, but it may be too soon to write off his plans as cosmetic and insubstantial. Analysis of the new party program and of the major speeches at the Congress suggests, in fact, that Gorbachev may be attempting to attack the problems in a realistic and systematic manner, given the nature of the Soviet system and the legacies he has inherited from his predecessors.

SOVIET PROBLEMS IN HISTORICAL PERSPECTIVE

The Stalinist legacy may be the most difficult to overcome, for it has shaped the institutions and the assumptions by which the Soviet Union is governed. Determined to forge a modern industrial state, Stalin built his party and state bureaucracies with persons utterly loyal to himself, and he used this power elite as the instrument of terror by which the population could be bludgeoned into fulfilling its assigned roles. His approach was narrowly effective, for it both generated a dramatic increase in industrial production and enforced a social revolution. The early five-year plans, however, established patterns of behavior and of relations between bureaucracy and public that have become impediments to further growth. In particular, Stalin entrusted the central planning apparatus—Gosplan and the economic ministries—with authority over every aspect of production.

This Stalinist heritage continues to cast a shadow over Soviet economic and social development. As Gorbachev observed at the Party Congress,

The forms of production relations and the economic management and guidance system now in operation took shape, basically, in the conditions of extensive economic development. These gradually grew out of date, began to lose their stimulating effect and in some respects became a brake.[2]

Faced with quotas and even detailed specifications for products and procedures, factory managers have had no latitude for innovation in design or work management. Soviet manufactured goods have earned their reputation for poor quality and design. Workers, too, are expected to fulfill hours on production quotas, with little incentive to go beyond the minimum requirements; indifference and apathy have not been uncommon in the Soviet work place. Perhaps the most important Stalinist legacy, however, has been an unimaginative leadership in party and government that has resisted changing the system, whether from lethargy or for fear of losing perquisites or simple suspicion of change.

Khrushchev's de-Stalinization speech of February 25, 1956, precisely thirty years before the opening of the 27th Party Congress, attacked the central symbols of the Stalinist system, but left alone the system itself. The very secrecy of his speech ensured that the audience was narrowly defined, limited to those "official" Soviets whose careers had been harnessed to the Stalinist system. Khrushchev may have grasped intuitively what the Soviet Union needed; he eased censorship, curtailed the Gulag, opened virgin lands to cultivation, and haltingly introduced some market-driven production. But Khrushchev lacked a program of reform; he relied upon first one, then another gimmick without systematic discipline. Perhaps more importantly, he was part of a generation of leadership whose careers had prospered under the Stalinist system and who distrusted major alterations of that system. Khrushchev fell in October 1964 for several reasons, including the inconsistency of his policies and the implicit threat to the system that his tinkering offered. The coup that ousted him installed a most conservative regime that bureaucrats and apparatchiki at every level could embrace.

The Brezhnev regime, committed from the start to perpetuating the system, demonstrated that the old ways retained sufficient vitality to drive economic growth, provide military needs, and sustain social stability for an additional twenty years. The cost has been exceedingly high: entrenched bureaucratic satrapies, aging plant, low productivity, and technological backwardness. Gorbachev may not have been merely seeking a scapegoat when he wrote in the party program that

> the 1970s and early 1980s saw certain unfavorable trends and difficulties in the country's development. To a great extent these were due to the failure to assess appropriately and in good time changes in the economic situation and the need for profound transformations in all spheres of life, and to a lack of persistence in carrying them out.[3]

Given the nature of the system and the legacies Gorbachev has inherited, the formidable challenges he faces must be attacked on at least three different fronts. (1) He must reduce the bureaucratic inhibitions to innovation that derive from the extraordinary power of the central planning apparatus, while at the same time retaining the loyalty and support of those bureaucrats and apparatchiki whose personal power may be threatened by the introduction of more extensive local initiative. (2) He must inspire in the citizenry a positive commitment to conservation of resources and efficiency through incentives for work and an improved selection of available consumer goods, but he cannot afford to divert capital from plant modernization and development of technological innovations in the factory. (3) He must reallocate capital into these areas without unduly antagonizing the many powerful functionaries in armaments, plant construction, and the military who are committed by career and ideology to continued growth in their own bailiwicks.

THE IMPLICATIONS OF THE REFORM PACKAGE

The more dramatic the reforms Gorbachev introduces in any given area, the more drastic are likely to be the political repercussions. Traditionally, the economic bureaucracy has exercised significant control over monthly and even daily management of individual factories. If their role becomes more focused upon policy guidelines, as Gorbachev has indicated, the political control of those bodies over regional and local functionaries will be reduced. To press institutional change without preparing the political base will guarantee failure for the reforms and weaken Gorbachev's own position. Apparatchiki and bureaucrats must support reform enthusiastically; those who cannot be persuaded will have to be replaced, a process already begun. During his first year, Gorbachev demoted or transferred hundreds of party officials and state bureaucrats, replacing them with more reform-minded people. The Central Committee of the CPSU, for example, is now dominated by "new" men.[4]

If his program is to succeed, Gorbachev must also devise a political strategy that will inspire in the working public a degree of enthusiasm and commitment that has seldom been found in the Soviet workplace. Gorbachev appears reluctant to rely heavily upon raw force to achieve his political goals, perhaps realizing that force would risk reinforcing the passivity and apathy of workers and plant managers. He also seems to realize that words, however stirring or candid, can hardly be expected to rally a public long inured to heavy-handed propaganda. The highly publicized attacks on corruption, accompanied by actual arrests, may be designed both to purge the system of malefactors and potential opponents and to persuade the public that the leadership is determined to bring fundamental change. Similarly, the spate of letters and articles in recent months that uncharacteristically criticize bureaucratic personnel and policies, often quite candidly, suggest at least the appearance of responsiveness to a measure of public opinion.

Gorbachev himself quite openly discussed the problems facing the USSR in his five-and-a-half hour speech opening the 27th Party Congress. He told the 5,000 delegates and 154 foreign observers that the past fifteen years of "negative processes" and "half-truth" can be overcome only with "considerable effort, time, and the loftiest sense of responsibility." The party must convince working people to embrace the needed reforms, and it must "restructure the psychology" of management and party apparatchiki.[5] Gorbachev clearly used the Congress to launch a revitalization of Soviet society and economy, based upon the proposals outlined in the Program, which the Congress adopted, and the major speeches, particularly his own and that of Nicholai Ryzhkov, new Chairman of the Council of Ministers, or prime minister.

Gorbachev proposed ambitious economic targets for the year

2000: a twofold increase in national income, a 250 percent increase in labor productivity, and reductions in energy and metal consumption of 28.6 and 50 percent, respectively. His projections would require a sustained growth rate of about 4.5 percent annually for these fifteen years, compared to the rate in recent years of about 3.2 percent.[6] Agricultural production is to double during the same period. The reforms necessary to achieve these goals, however, seem to be less profound than many Western observers expected, consisting primarily of a new investment strategy, intensive development of silicon technology, increased economic incentives, broader application of cost accounting, and increased efficiency and conservation of scarce resources.

The proposed new investment strategy promises a transition from the previously dominant emphasis upon construction of new facilities to the retooling and modernization of outmoded plants. Considerable attention is to be given to technologically advanced production, including computers, automation, and robotics. One consequence of automation is expected to be a 50 percent reduction of jobs in manual labor. In addition, the scientific community stands to benefit from increased monies poured into research and development of economically feasible technologies. This push toward automation and increased computer applications will be extremely difficult to achieve, given the backwardness of the Soviet computer industry, the scarcity of basic programming software, and the shortage of instructional personnel well versed in computer use.

The heart of Gorbachev's economic program is to be found in his related proposals for new incentives and cost accounting, which require *"reorganization of the work of the central economic bodies, first and foremost, the State Planning Committee of the USSR."*[7] In particular, Gorbachev insists that the central bureaucracy must cease its "interference" in the daily activities of factories. Each productive unit, whether industrial or agricultural, will be responsible for achieving income sufficient to cover capital and operating costs. Successful enterprises will be allowed to sell surplus production and dispose of the profit as they see fit. Consistent losses in a factory may be expected to bring a change in management and perhaps close down the enterprise altogether. Factory personnel, particularly management, will be held responsible, for example, if their consumer goods do not sell because of poor design, sloppy workmanship, or low demand. Collective and state farms will be assessed a tax to be paid in produce; surpluses may be consumed or sold to the state or other consumers. Prices will be based upon costs and demand, and payrolls "should be directly tied in with the returns from the sale of its products."[8]

These innovations, which are vaguely reminiscent of the New Economic Policy that Lenin adopted in 1921, would create a limited market economy and go far toward dismantling the most cumbersome aspects of Stalinist-style central planning. But they will not be implemented easily. Rigorous application of cost accounting often encounters political opposition, as it has in the military procurement system in the United States. Gorbachev is in effect threatening many thousands of industrial and agricultural managers with an ultimatum: either produce for the market or lose your job. One wonders whether the Soviets will be seeking American advice on defining the market and promoting the product.

Gorbachev emphasized, perhaps optimistically, the economic gains that can come from reducing waste, increasing labor productivity through harder work, and conservation of resources. He stated that almost all of the economic growth in 1986 will come from these efforts. The problems of inefficiency that he hopes to solve, however, are more deeply rooted in habits of work and management than in organizational structure or technology. Perhaps the habits and attitudes can be overcome by exhortation and punishment—crusading against alcoholism, attacking absenteeism and lax work performance, arresting white-collar criminals, and rewarding exemplary workers. The pervasiveness of these problems, however, justifies a degree of skepticism that solutions can be found quickly.

The general secretary informed his compatriots in blunt terms that unless they apply themselves enthusiastically to the economic reforms, there will be little improvement in the standard of living. Conversely, he predicted that success will bring a number of enticing consequences. Real per capita incomes will rise as much as 80 percent by the end of the century, welfare funds will be increased, education will be much more richly funded, consumer goods of high quality will be more readily available, more people will be nudged into service jobs (housekeepers, mechanics, repairmen), more housing will be built, and improved medical services will be provided.[9]

These social goals point to several of the major areas in which ordinary Soviet citizens have been forced to cope with inadequate resources. Prominent figures in party, government, academia, sport, culture, and military, however, have long had access to special services and stores, and they have received preferential access to education and cultural events. The propriety of these privileges became the subject of reportedly heated debate at the Congress.

Boris Yeltsin, new party boss in Moscow and member of the Politburo, criticized abuses of the perquisites in his speech. He argued that party leaders who have been seduced by their privileges to abandon modesty and selflessness are "the source of the decay of the Party and the lowering of Communist authority." On the other hand, Yegor Ligachev, a member of both the Secretariat and the Politburo, defended preferential treatment for those leaders who had earned them. He even rebuked *Pravda* editor Viktor Afanasiev, a member of the Central Committee, for publishing letters that were too strongly critical of the special stores.[10] Gorbachev treated the issue gingerly; he supported Ligachev's attack on "petty dirty-linen-washing," but he also insisted that "the distribution of benefits should be so organized . . . that every Soviet citizen should have firm faith in our ideals and values."[11]

The party seems to face a dilemma: continuance of the system of privileged access to services and goods may undermine public faith in the party, but the elite is not likely to accept with equanimity any considerable reduction in its perks. Of course, if the economic plan succeeds in providing high-quality industrial and agricultural products, decent health care, adequate housing, and all the other targeted improvements, then the special facilities should arouse less criticism.

Yet another dilemma received attention at the Congress: the relationship between foreign policy and economic reforms.[12] Foreign trade, particularly with "developed capitalist states," must be increased in order to introduce the technological improvements that the economic plan envisions. Increased trade with the West, however, requires less volatile political relations than those of the past decade.[13] As might be expected, Gorbachev blamed the threats to world peace upon "the policy of military force" embraced by the United States, and he promised that the Soviet Union will not settle for less security than it now has. He affirmed his desire for "the lowest possible level of strategic parity" between the USSR and the United States, which would exclude nuclear weapons altogether, but he pledged to maintain parity at whatever level is necessary.[14]

Easing world tensions and reducing the arms race are also important to the Soviets because the economic plan will require vast sums for modernizing old plants, creating a computer industry, improving social services, and the rest. The continuing high level of military and arms expenditures diverts resources from areas that would be more productive, and efforts to counter the "Star Wars" program of the United States promise to increase the drain of funds by far greater amounts than would be freed by disengagement from Afghanistan, which Gorbachev hopes to effect.[15]

Reduction of arms, of course, must be negotiated with the United States, some of whose traditional demands Gorbachev has offered to meet. The moratorium on underground testing, coupled with a proposed comprehensive test ban treaty seems to embrace a major goal of U.S. policy sought by every president from Eisenhower to Carter and rejected by Khrushchev and Brezhnev. Perhaps more impressive is Gorbachev's endorsement of on-site verification of disarmament procedures, a U.S. demand that his predecessors refused to countenance.[16] In addition to these seeming concessions, Gorbachev also called upon public opinion in the West—the peace movement—to pressure NATO governments to negotiate arms reductions on terms that do not disadvantage the USSR.

Should the Soviet Union and the United States achieve significant progress toward reducing nuclear arms through a negotiated and mutually ratified treaty, Gorbachev would profit enormously. His credibility within the USSR would be greatly enhanced, to the extent that he might be able to translate public enthusiasm into a crusade for his economic reforms. He could allocate to reforms a portion of the budget previously designated for nuclear arms research and construction. He also would gain internationally, for existing trade barriers against the USSR would be difficult to maintain in the aftermath of such a treaty. It should not be surprising that Gorbachev has strongly emphasized his "peace initiative."

CONCLUSIONS: PROSPECTS FOR SUCCESS

Mikhail Gorbachev put on a bravura performance in the Party Congress. He acknowledged the problems facing his country, and while his solutions leave intact the broad structures of the Soviet system, they do call for sweeping new policies. He also presented an aura of determined optimism in the face of difficult and complex tasks ahead, a posture no doubt calculated to rekindle faith in what can be achieved through hard work and dedication. The ultimate question remains: can new policies, optimism, and faith suffice to revive the Soviet economy, or is the system so fundamentally flawed, so susceptible to corruption and inefficiency, that it will defeat even the most determined efforts at reform?

During his last, convalescing year, Lenin complained bitterly that rule-bound, inflexible bureaucrats were impeding progress toward the just, humane society. Stalin, who constructed a system far more bureaucratic and far less humane than that against which the "old man" had railed, consistently accused "wreckers" and "saboteurs" when the five-year plans fell short of their goals. In his turn, Khrushchev blamed the ills of the Soviet Union upon Stalin, and with good cause; but he failed to overcome the most glaring deficiencies, some of which (namely alcoholism, labor productivity, and agricultural productivity) actually worsened. Brezhnev and his cohorts, holding Khrushchev responsible for continuing shortcomings, purported to abandon his innovations in favor of conservative, centralized management of the economy and society. Perhaps Gorbachev merely continues the tradition by which the new leader accuses his predecessor of errors or even heresy and offers himself as the redeemer who will restore the true faith and lead his people into the promised era of plenty and justice. However sincerely dedicated to reform, Gorbachev may be blinded by ideology to the essential bankruptcy of a system that no amount of tinkering can fix.

Unfortunately, ideological myopia may also be the source of assertions that the proposed reforms are doomed by their superficiality. It would be premature, indeed, to pass final judgment on Gorbachev's program before it has had a chance to unfold. The pitfalls are many and deep, but it is hardly clear that they cannot be avoided.

The new leader recognizes that the system inherited from Stalin must be overhauled if it is to function at an acceptable level, and he seems fully aware that his reforms imply that the old style of political and social control must be abandoned. The prospect is daunting, but Gorbachev has an unprecedented opportunity to replace the conservative old guard at every level with reform-minded younger leaders; if this new generation can be persuaded that its own self-interest dictates support for the reforms, then the prognosis improves dramatically. Of course, the general public must also be persuaded that cynicism no longer is warranted, a feat that will probably require concrete evidence of improvement in the short run.

Students of Soviet politics rightly discount the popular assumption that the general secretary wields total authority, but he certainly does have cardinal influence, thanks to his control of patronage, of policy formulation, and of a "bully pulpit" from which to articulate his ideas. The most effective political leaders are those who can manipulate the levers of power while persuading their citizens to share a common vision. Gorbachev has already demonstrated sufficiently impressive talents in both areas that his program of reform should not yet be relegated to the "ash heap of history."

NOTES

1. Seweryn Bialer and Joan Afferica, "The genesis of Gorbachev's world," *Foreign Affairs: America and the World, 1985* 64, No. 3 (February 1986), p. 605ff.; Marshall I. Goldman, "Gorbachev and economic reform," *Foreign Affairs* 64, No. 1 (Fall 1985), pp. 58ff.; Seweryn Bialer,

"Gorbachev: Much talk, little action," *U.S. News and World Report* (March 17, 1986), p. 38.
   2. Mikhail Gorbachev, "Political report of the CPSU Central Committee to the 27th Party Congress." (Moscow: Novosti Press Agency Publishing House, 1986), p. 43.
   3. *The Programme of the Communist Party of the Soviet Union* (Moscow: Novosti Press Agency Publishing House, 1986), p. 27.
   4. For a good discussion of the personnel changes Gorbachev has effected, see Archie Brown, "Change in the Soviet Union," *Foreign Affairs* 64, No. 4 (Summer 1986), pp. 1048ff.
   5. Gorbachev, "Political Report," op. cit., p. 27.
   6. Nikolai Ryzhkov, "Guidelines for the economic and social development of the USSR for 1986–1990 and for the period ending in 2000," (Moscow: Novosti Press Agency Publishing House, 1986), p. 15; Gary Thatcher, "Gorbachev seen as overhauling Soviet economy," *Christian Science Monitor* (Oct. 17, 1985), p. 7.
   7. Gorbachev, "Political Report," op. cit., p. 39. (Emphasis in the original.)
   8. Ibid., p. 41.
   9. Ibid., p. 56–58.
   10. Gary Lee, "Party members' perks make some see Red in Moscow," *Washington Post* (March 3, 1986), p. A13.
   11. Gorbachev, "Political Report," op. cit., p. 98.
   12. An interesting discussion of this issue may be found in Sidney I. Ploss, "A new Soviet era?" *Foreign Policy* (Spring, 1986), pp. 45ff.
   13. Ryzhkov, "Guidelines," op. cit., p. 52.
   14. Gorbachev, "Political Report," op. cit., p. 76.
   15. Ibid., p. 79.
   16. Ibid., p. 75–77.

Recommended Readings

BOOKS

Baradat, Leon P. *Soviet Political Society.* Englewood Cliffs, NJ: Prentice-Hall, 1986.

Barghoorn, Frederick C. and Thomas F. Remington. *Politics in the USSR.* Boston: Little, Brown and Company, 1986.

Barry, Donald D. and Carol Barner-Barry. *Contemporary Soviet Politics.* Third edition. Englewood Cliffs, NJ: Prentice-Hall, 1987.

Byrnes, Robert F. (ed.) *After Brezhnev: Sources of Soviet Conduct in the 1980s.* Bloomington: Indiana University Press, 1983.

Colton, Timothy J. *The Dilemma of Reform in the Soviet Union.* Revised edition. New York: Council on Foreign Relations, 1986.

Dallin, Alexander and Condoleezza Rice (eds.). *The Gorbachev Era. (The Portable Stanford).* Stanford, CA: Stanford Alumni Association, 1986.

Gorbachev, Mikhail S., *Speeches and Writings.* New York: Pergamon Books, Inc., 1986.

Hammer, Darrell P. *The USSR: The Politics of Oligarchy*, Second edition. Boulder, CO: Westview Press, 1986.

Medish, Vadim. *The Soviet Union.* Third edition. Englewood Cliffs, NJ: Prentice-Hall, 1987.

Medvedev, Zhores. *Gorbachev.* New York: W. W. Norton & Company, 1986.

Nogee, Joseph L. (ed.). *Soviet Politics: Russia After Brezhnev*. New York: Praeger, 1985.
Parks, Michelle and John L. Moore, (eds). *The Soviet Union*. Second edition. Washington: Congressional Quarterly Inc., 1986.
Schmidt-Häuer, Christian. *Gorbachev: The Path to Power*, trans. E. Osers and C. Romberg, edited by John Man. Topfield, MA: Salem House, 1986.

JOURNAL ARTICLES

Bialer, Seweryn and Joan Afferica. "The Genesis of Gorbachev's World," *Foreign Affairs: America and the World 1985*. Vol 64, No. 3 (February 1986), pp. 605–644.
Brown, Archie. "Change in the Soviet Union," *Foreign Affairs* 64, No. 1 (Summer 1986), pp. 1048–65.
Brown, Archie. "Gorbachev: New Man in the Kremlin," *Problems of Communism* 34 (May–June 1985), pp. 1–23.
Goodman, Elliot R. "Gorbachev Takes Charge: Prospects for Soviet Society," *Survey* 29, No. 2 (Summer 1985 [sic—actually 1986)], pp. 180–201.
Larrabee, F. Stephen and Allen Lynch, "Gorbachev: The Road to Reykjavik," *Foreign Policy* 65 (Winter 1986–87), pp. 3–28.
Lendvai, Paul. "Who is Afraid of Mikhail Gorbachev?" *Survey* 29, No. 2 (Summer 1985 [sic—actually 1986]), pp. 202–217.
Ploss, Sidney I. "A New Soviet Era?" *Foreign Policy* 62 (Spring 1986), pp. 46–60.
Simes, Dimitri K. "Gorbachev: A New Foreign Policy?" *Foreign Affairs: America and the World 1986*, Vol 65, No. 3 (February 1987), pp. 477–500.
"The Soviet Union, 1985." *Current History* 84, No. 504 (November, 1985), entire issue.
"The Soviet Union, 1986." *Current History* 85, No. 513 (October, 1986), entire issue.

Index

academic institutes, 26
Academy of Sciences, USSR, 39, 63
Afanasiev, Viktor, 145
Afferica, Joan, 14
Afghanistan, 57, 138, 146; Gorbachev's policy, 67–68
Aganbegyan, Abel, 86
agriculture (*see* economy)
alcohol, alcoholism: campaign against, 13, 25–26, 74, 81, 91, 101–2, 121–22
Alexander II, 46
Alexander III, 56
Andropov, Yuri, 18, 19, 25, 76, 101, 138; age, 2; appointees, 13; leadership style, 34; party bureaucracy, 8; patronage, 40; president or head of state, 10; reform policies, 47; term of office, 1
Angola, 28, 61; Soviet intervention, 67
anti-Semitism, Soviet, 128–29
Arab–Israeli conflict, 61

Arbatov, Georgi, 23–24
arms control, 29–31; Gorbachev proposals, 13 (*see also* Gorbachev)
art, avant-garde, 125, 130
Aswan Dam (*see* Egypt)

Babii Yar, 129
Baikal Amur (BAM), 79
Baikal-Amur railroad, 79, 89
Bakaa Valley: Syrian-Israeli air battle, 65
Belorussia, 107
Bialer, Seweryn, 14, 138
Birynkov, Aleksandra, 9
Bogomolov, Oleg, 99, 100, 112
Bolshevik Revolution, 123
Bolsheviks, 123–24; as revolutionary intellectuals, 59; survivers, 46
Brezhnev, Leonid, 18, 22, 74, 101, 102–3, 117, 138, 140, 146, 147; age, 2; appointees, 9, 12; arms control, 62; backgrounds of appointees, 36; détente poli-

Brezhnev, Leonid (*continued*)
  cies, 50; general secretary, 11–12; patronage, 40; president or head of state, 10; relations with Khrushchev, 8, 10; Soviet economy, 13, 14; term of office, 2
bribes, 103, 110–11
brigade method, 109
Bukharin, Nikolai, 123
Bulgakov, Mikhail, 130–31
bureaucracy, 76–77, 85–86, 139, 140–41, 143, 147; party, 5–6, 12, 14; state, 5, 12, 14

cabinet, Soviet (*see* Council of Ministers)
Carter, Jimmy, 62
Castro, Fidel, 67
Central America, 61; Castro and Soviet Union, 67
Central Committee of the Communist Party, 3, 76, 101, 111, 145; backgrounds of members, 35–36; economic reform, 44; functions, 6; general secretary, 6; Gorbachev appointees, 9, 50, 142; membership, 6; recruitment, 40–41; rise of Gorbachev, 41–42; Secretariat, 5, 8, 12
Central Intelligence Agency (CIA), 70
Central Statistical Administration, 100
Cherenenko, Konstantin, 18, 20, 101, 138; age, 2; appointees, 13; arms control, 62; background of appointees, 37; Khadafy visit to Soviet Union, 67; member of old guard, 35; Presidium of the Supreme Soviet, 44; party and state, 45;
  patronage, 40; president or head of state, 10; term of office, 1–2, 3
Chernobyl, 96, 99–100, 133, 134
China, 28, 30, 109; economic reforms, 13; nuclear weapons and Soviet Union, 64; relations with Soviet Union, 68
Clayton, Elizabeth, 114
"commanding heights" of industry, 88
Communist Party of the Soviet Union (CPSU): barrier to reform, 47, 51–52; comparison with American and Western European parties, 4; general secretary, 5; party program, 13, 52, 60, 138, 142; recruitment of leaders, 5–6, 39–40
constitution, Soviet: functions of Supreme Soviet, 9
conventional weapons: Soviet perspectives, 66, 71; U.S.–Soviet balance, 65
correlation of forces, 60
Council of Ministers, 101; administration of Politburo policies, 12; ages of members, 35–36; backgrounds of members, 37; chairman of the Presidium (prime minister), 5, 11; membership and functions, 10–11; presidium, 11
Council for Mutual Economic Assistance (COMECON/CMEA), 75, 90, 99
Cuba: missile crisis of 1962, 8 (*see also* Spain)
culture, cultural policy, 121, 124–25, 127, 130; American indifference to, 60–61; pre-revolutionary, 123–24; prospects for change, 130; revolutionary,

124–25; Soviet, 125, 129–30, 131; Soviet, post-Stalinist, 126, 128; Stalinist, 125–26, 131; under Gorbachev, 131–34
Czechoslovakia: Soviet invasion of in 1968, 130

Damascus, Syria, 58, 61
de Tocqueville, Alexis, 69
détente, 49–50
Dobrynin, Anatoly: appointed to Secretariat by Gorbachev, 9; background, 48
Dolgikh, Vladimir, 41, 45; Central Committee secretary, 34
Dostoevsky, Fedor, 124
Dr. Zhivago, 126
drama, Soviet, 130–31
Dzerzhinsky, Feliks, 59

Eastern Europe, 27, 28, 75, 99
economy, economic policies, 27, 100; agriculture, 43–44, 52, 74, 78, 80–81, 88, 91; assistance to developing countries, 75; balance of payments/trade, 75–76; bonuses, 91–92; centralized planning, 88–89; Chernobyl, 99–100; construction, 79; consumer services, consumerism, 75, 79, 81, 86, 90, 97–99; corruption, 91; criticism by Soviets, 122–23; currency, 99; decentralization, 74, 84–85, 88, 91; discipline, 27, 78, 81, 91, 100–103, 107, 115; education, 98; Eastern Europe, 75, 99, 100; efficiency, 78, 79–80, 89; energy, 74–75, 88; exports, 75; Gorbachev reforms, 12–13, 43, 44, 48, 69; GNP in 1985, 74–75; growth, 74–75, 79; hard currency reserves, 75; health, 98; housing, 84–82, 98, 112–13; imports, 75, 87; incentives, 78–79, 81–82, 87, 89–92, 102–3, 113–14; income, 81, 90, 91; industrial renovation, 79–80; initiative, 111; intensification, 77–79, 84, 89–92; investment, 75–76, 78–80; job security, 77, 115; leadership accountability, 88–90; machine building, 75, 78–80, 88, 90; machine imports, 74; military effects, 30, 70, 75, 92–93; motivation, 102; Party Congress (*see* Party Congress [27th]); planning, 74–75, 97–100; prices, 84; private enterprise, privatization, 109–11; privilege, 90; productivity, 27, 98–100, 102; resource allocation, 27, 74, 77; robotics, 83; salaries and wages, 90–91, 98, 112; state intervention, 100; subsidies, 86; technology, 82–84, 87, 90, 92, 98; wages (*see* economy, salaries, above); weather, 99; West, influence of/on, 61, 75–76, 83, 92, 99
education, 103–6, 112–13
Egypt, 58
Ehrenburg, Ilya, 127
energy, 77–78
equality (*see* social justice)
espionage, 83

Fifteen Year Plan (1986–2000), 74–75, 97
Five Year Plan, 12th (1986–1900), 74, 97–100
foreign policy: general, 25, 28–29 (*see also* Gorbachev)
France: Gorbachev visit, 13; nuclear weapons, 62

gas (*see* economy; energy)
general secretary (*see* Central Committee; Communist Party)
Geneva summit meeting, 21, 23, 29–30, 31, 96
Germany: Marxist prediction of revolution, 59
gerontocracy, 2
Goldman, Marshall, 138
Gorbachev, Mikhail, 138–39, 141–48; age, 1–3, 18, 21–22, 96; appointees, 12–13, 26, 40, 50; arms control, 62, 63, 64, 66, 70, 146–47; assumption of power in 1985, 1, 2, 21; attitude toward military, 61–62; background, 18–20, 23, 41–42, 43–44, 46; economic reforms, 14, 44, 52, 69, 90, 139, 142–45; education, 3, 103; foreign policy, 13, 27–29; 49, 56, 62, 67, 68, 71–72; head of party/general secretary, 5; impact on Soviet Union, 51; leadership style, 22–23, 24–25, 31; partocracy, 45; party and state, 44–45, 52; party bureaucracy, 8–9; Party Congress (27th), 20, 21, 142, 145; party program, 141; policies (general), 25; potential opposition to, 21, 76, 90, 122–23; prospects for change under, 27, 31, 116–17; reforms (general), 41, 46–52; relations with Castro, 67
Gorbachev, Raisa, 2, 24, 62
Gorbachev generation, 34–38, 148; backgrounds, 35–38, 41, 48; economic reforms, 50–52; foreign policy, 50; goals, 35; impact on Soviet Union, 51; reforms, 46–47
Gosplan, 79

Great Britain: Gorbachev visit, 48; Marxist prediction of revolution, 59; nuclear forces, 62; parties and prime minister, 4
Gregory, Paul, 116
Gromyko, Andrei, 28; appointment as president of Soviet Union, 8; member of old guard, 34–35; membership in Politburo, 10; president or head of state, 10

Hamlet, 130
head of state, Soviet, 10 (*see also* Presidium of Supreme Soviet)
higher educational institutions (VUZy), 105–6
Hitler, Adolf, 126
House of Representatives, U.S.: comparison with Supreme Soviet, 4, 9
humor, Soviet, 122
Hungary, 8, 110; economic reforms, 13, 110

ideology, Soviet: Bolshevik intellectuals, 59–60; Soviet Union today, 60; diminished appeal, 58–59, 60; Gorbachev reforms, 13–14; leadership recruitment, 37; Soviet economy, 46–47
India: Soviet aid to, 58; Soviet trade with, 58
inequalities (*see* Social justice)
intelligentsia, 123–24, 126
Iran, 66–67
Iraq, 66–67
Israel, 61, 65
Izvestia, 101, 133

Japan, 28, 78–79; relations with Soviet Union, 68

Kalashnikov, V. I., 86
Kandinsky, Vasily, 124-25
Kazakhstan, 85
Kennedy, John, 127; John and Jackie, 2
KGB (*see* secret police)
Khadafy, Omar, 64, 67; visit to Soviet Union, 67
Khrushchev, Nikita, 18, 22, 86, 96, 115, 122, 123, 140, 146, 147; age, 2; chairman, Council of Ministers, 11-12; "cult of personality," 8; economic reforms, 46-47; general secretary/first secretary, 5, 6-8, 11-12; leadership style, 62; party bureaucracy, 6-8; Politburo/Presidium of CPSU, 5; relationship to Brezhnev, 10; removal from office, 47; secret speech at 20th Party Congress, 8, 21; Soviet economy, 13; term of office, 2
Kiev, 128-29
Kissinger, Henry, 50
Kolbin, Gennadi, 85
kolkhoz, 24, 91
komsomol, 39, 42
Kostakis, George, 125
Kostakov, Vladimir, 108, 110
Kosygin, Aleksei: chairman, Council of Ministers/prime minister, 11-12; relations with Khrushchev, 8
Krasnodar, 77, 91
Krupskaya, Nadezhda, 24
Kulakov, Fedor, 19
Kunayev, Dinmukhamed, 85
Kurile Islands, 28 (*see also* Japan)

labor, labor policies, 79, 106; brigade or team system, 84-85, 109; challenges, 107, 108-9; dismissals, 107; job security, 78, 106-9; pensioners, 89; personal and family contributions, 84-85, 89, 91, 109; productivity, 78, 79, 81, 87, 89-90, 108; service employment, 108; shortages, 78, 107; utilization, 78, 79-81, 84, 89, 107
Lebanon (*see* Bakaa Valley)
leaders, Soviet: ages, 2-3; attitudes toward military force, 57-58; backgrounds, 36-38, 48; current ages, 35; economic reform, 52; expertise gap, 49; foreign policy, 48; goals under Gorbachev, 35; ideology today, 60; implications of reforms, 47-48; nuclear forces, 71; party, 5-6; patronage, 8, 40; promotions, 37; recruitment, 34, 38-41; state, 5-6
Lenin, Vladimir, 22, 25, 80, 91, 123-24, 125, 147; as a Bolshevik intellectual, 59; death of, 6; exile in West, 59; New Economic Policy (NEP), 46-47, 144; term of office, 2
Lenin Agricultural Academy, 76-77
Levikov, Aleksandr, 38-40
Libya, 67
Ligachev, Yegor, 9, 90, 116, 145
Lisitsky, Eliezer (El), 124-25
literature, Soviet, 125-30 (*see also* culture, Soviet)
Literaturnaya Gazeta, 38, 132-33
Lyubimov, Yuri, 130-31

Macbeth, 130
McClellan, Woodford, 31
Machine-Building Bureau, 76 (*see also* economy, machine building)
Malevich, Kazimir, 124-25

Mandelshtam, Josip, 127
Markov, Georgi, 60–61
Marx, Karl, 59
Marxism-Leninism, 35 (see also ideology)
Master and Margarita, The, 130–31
Mayakovsky, Vladimir, 125, 128
Mexico, 57
Mexico City, 133–34
Middle East, 28
Millar, James, 115
military, Soviet, 49, 61 (see also economy, military effects)
Moscow, 82, 131
Moscow Art Theater, 131
Murakhovskiy, Vsevolod S., 76–77, 80–81, 91

NATO, 49
Net Material Product, 74–75
New Economic Policy (NEP), 46–47, 80, 144
New York Times, 132–33
Nicaragua, 28, 67
Nicholas II, 56
Nikonov, A. A., 76–77
Nixon, Richard, 50, 61–62, 122
nomenklatura, 38, 85–86
nuclear weapons, 62–65, 70–71

oblasts, 36
oil exports, 99

partocracy, 35, 36–38, 39–40, 41, 44–45, 47, 52
party/parties: democratic/ Western, 4; Polish Socialist Party, 59; Soviet/ Communist, 3–5; Swiss and German socialist parties, 59
Party Congress, 6, 9, 20; 16th (1927), 86; 20th (1956), 8, 13, 20, 86; 22nd (1961), 86; 27th (1986), 6, 9, 20, 50, 51–52, 60, 76, 83–84, 87, 89, 96, 100, 103, 109, 112, 116, 134, 138–42, 145–47 [Gorbachev and, 9, 22, 74, 77, 109, 111]; 28th (1991), 86; membership and functions of, 6
Pasternak, Boris, 126–27, 135
patronage, 40
pensioners (see labor)
Peredelkino, 126–27
personnel changes, 26, 76, 85–86
Philippines, 57
Podgorny, Nikolai, 8, 10
Poland, 8, 57
Politburo, 3, 4–5, 76, 110–11, 145; ages of members, 2; Andropov appointees, 8; general policymaking functions, 12; Gorbachev appointees, 8–9, 50; Gorbachev appointments, 9; members and candidate members, 5–6; new appointees, 34; Party Congress, 6; Presidium, 5; recruitment, 40, 41–42; rise of Gorbachev, 41–42
Popova, Lyubov, 124–25
post-industrialism, 108
Pravda, 101, 110–11, 116, 133
"president" of the Soviet Union, 10 (see also head of state; Presidium of the Supreme Soviet)
Presidium of the Supreme Soviet, 10 (see also head of state; Supreme Soviet)
press, Soviet, 133–34 (see also *Izvestia; Pravda;* TASS)
Priezzhaev, Nikolai, 44–45
prime minister, Soviet, 11–12 (see also Council of Ministers)
proletkult, 125
public morality, Soviet, 102

public opinion, Soviet, 100–101, 103, 114, 122–23, 130, 131–32; emigrés, 114–15
purges, 18
Pushkin, Aleksander, 124, 128

Radek, Karl, 59
Reagan, Ronald, 2, 13, 21, 23–24, 29–30, 82, 138; arms control, 63; and Strategic Defense Initiative, 29, 63, 82 (*see also* Geneva summit meeting; Strategic Defense Initiative), 110
republics, Soviet: representation in Supreme Soviet, 9
Reykjavik summit meeting, 30, 63
robotics, 83
Rodchenko, Aleksander, 124–25
Romanenko, G. A., 77
Romanov, Grigori, 3, 8
Ryzhkov, Nikolai, 45, 79–80, 81, 83–84, 90, 100, 142; background, 41; chairman of Council of Ministers (prime minister), 9, 12; economic reform, 52; membership in Politburo, 34; speech to 27th Party Congress, 74, 79–80, 81

samagon (privately brewed alcohol), 102
samizdat, 133
Savimbi, Jonas, 67
Schmemann, Serge, 132
SDI (*see* Strategic Defense Initiative)
secondary vocational-technical schools (SPTUs), 104–6
secret police (KGB), 5, 47
Secretariat, 76; ages of members, 35; party bureaucracy, 12–13

(*see also* Central Committee, general secretary)
secretaries, party (*see* Secretariat)
Semichastny, Vladimir, 47
Senate, U.S.: comparison with Supreme Soviet, 4, 9
Shakespeare, William, 130
Shchekino chemical complex, 106
Shcherbitsky, Vladimir, 85
Shelepin, Alexander, 8
Shevardnadze, Eduard, 8–9, 10, 68
Sibaral Canal, 79
Simes, Dimitri, 123
social justice, Soviet, 109, 112–14, 115–16
social policies, Soviet, 84–85, 96, 109–10, 113, 116–17 (*see also* economy; education; labor)
socialism, advanced, 60
"socialism in one country," 25
Socialist Realism, 125, 126
South Korea, 78–79
South Yemen, 28, 58
Sovetskaya Kultura, 108
Soviet Interview Project, 114, 115 (see also public opinion, Soviet [emigrés])
Soviet of Nationalities (*see* Supreme Soviet)
Soviet of the Union (*see* Supreme Soviet)
Soviet Writers' Union (Moscow), 132
sovkhoz, 91
Spain, 57
Stalin, Joseph, 3, 18, 21, 22, 25, 115, 139–40, 144, 147; appointees, 46; arms control, 62; assumption of power, 2; chairman, Council of Ministers, 11, 12; general secretary of CPSU, 11; Party Congress, 6; Soviet

Stalin, Joseph (*continued*)
  economy, 13 (*see also* Culture)
  standard of living, Soviet, 86, 97, 98–99, 114
Stanislavsky, Konstantin, 131
Star Wars (*see* Strategic Defense Initiative)
state: Gorbachev, 9; Soviet, 3, 5–6, 9
State Agro-Industrial Committee, 76, 80–81, 91, 107
Stavropol, 24, 76–77
Strategic Defense Initiative (SDI), 29, 63, 82, 87
succession, Soviet political, 21–22
summit meeting (*see* Geneva summit meeting)
super-ministries, 76, 91
Supreme Soviet, 9, 23; comparison with Western parliaments, 4–5; functions, 9–10; membership, 9; Presidium, 10, 11
Suslov, Mikhail, 8, 19
Syria, 65–66

Taganka Theater (Moscow), 130–31
Talyzin, Nikolai, 79
Tashkent, 133–34
TASS, 108
Texas, 57
Thatcher, Margaret, 23
Terror, the, 124, 126
Thaw, The, 127–28
Third World, 28; elite interest in Soviet system of control, 59; Soviet aid to, 58; Soviet foreign policy, 49
Tikhonov, Nikolai, 9, 12, 34–35
Times (London), 131
Trotsky, Leon, 2, 123–24
Truman, Harry, 62

Ukraine, 85, 99–100, 129
United States, 144, 146; arms control, 66; nuclear and conventional weapons, 65; parties, 4; reaction to Gorbachev's foreign policy, 69; representative organs, 4; Soviet arms control proposals, 63; Soviet military threat, 61; Soviet relations with, 28, 29–32, 49–50, 60, 75, 87, 92; technology, 56, 58
Ustinov, Dimitri, 34–35

Vienna, Austria, 56–57
vocational-technical schools (PTUs), 104–5
Volgograd, 86
Vorotnikov, Vitaly, 34, 41, 45

Western Europe: cabinets, 11; Marxist predictions of revolution, 59; missiles, 62; parliamentary systems of, 10; parties, 4–5
Wharton School, 75
Wilson, Woodrow, 2
World War I, 59
World War II, 28, 57, 68, 128–29
writers, Soviet (*see* culture; literature)

Yeltsin, Boris, 82, 85, 86–87, 88, 89, 90, 145
Yevtushenko, Yevgeny, 128–29, 132–33
Yudovich, Lev, 43

Zaikov, Lev, 9
Zaslavskaya, Tatiana, 39, 40–41, 113
Zinoviev, Grigori, 124

About the Editors and Contributors

JEAN FARNETH BOONE is a senior research assistant in Soviet economics for the Congressional Research Service.

WALTER D. CONNOR is professor of political science and director of Soviet and East European Studies at Boston University. He is a Fellow of the Russian Research Center at Harvard and the author or co-author of three books on socialist societies and the Soviet Union. He served from 1976 to 1984 as Director of Soviet and East European Studies at the Foreign Service Institute of the Department of State. He is currently working on a study of workers and politics in post-Stalin USSR with support from the Guggenheim Foundation and the National Council for Soviet and East European Research.

ARTHUR B. GUNLICKS is professor of political science at the University of Richmond. He is the author of *Local Government in the German Federal System* (Duke University Press, 1986) and the contributing editor of *Local Government Reform and Reorganization: An International Perspective* (Kennikat Press/National University Publications, 1981). He has also written numerous articles and book chapters on German government and politics.

JOHN P. HARDT is senior specialist and associate director for senior specialists in Soviet economics of the Congressional Research Service. He has authored and edited numerous books and articles for commercial, government, and academic publications on East–West commercial relations and the economies of Eastern Europe, the Soviet Union, and the People's Republic of China.

J. MARTIN RYLE is professor of history at the University of Richmond, where he teaches courses in Soviet history and socialist thought. He has published on the subject of the Comintern in the 1920s, and he is currently working on a computer game simulation of the Russian Revolution of 1917.

DIMITRI K. SIMES received his advanced degrees from Moscow State University and the Institute of World Economy and International Relations, USSR Academy of Science. He is now a senior associate at the Carnegie Endowment for International Peace, a consultant for CBS News, and a columnist for the *Christian Science Monitor*. He is the author of numerous articles in leading American newspapers and journals, and he has authored or contributed to several books on Soviet foreign policy and U.S.–Soviet relations.

KONSTANTIN SIMIS was a member of the Moscow bar as a defense attorney and a professor for the higher diplomatic school in Moscow before emigrating to the United States. He is now a commentator for Radio Liberty broadcasts to the Soviet Union, and he writes and lectures on Soviet affairs. He is the author of *The USSR: The Corrupt Society* (Simon and Schuster, 1982).

HELMUT SONNENFELDT is a guest scholar at the Brookings Institution in Washington, D.C. After serving as a research and intelligence specialist in the Department of State, he became head of the Department's Office of Research and Analysis for the USSR and Eastern Europe. Before retiring from the Department of State in 1977, he was a senior staff member of the National Security Council and Counselor of the Department of State. He has published numerous articles on foreign affairs, and he appears frequently on radio and television as a commentator on international issues.

JOHN D. TREADWAY is an assistant professor of modern European history at the University of Richmond. He is the author of *The Falcon and the Eagle: Montenegro and Austria–Hungary, 1908–1914* (Purdue University Press, 1983), and of articles on the Balkans and modern Germany.

IRWIN WEIL is professor of Russian and Russian literature at Northwestern University. For many years he has been deeply involved in cultural exchange between the United States and the Soviet Union. He has published several works on Russian and Soviet literature and culture.

www.ingramcontent.com/pod-product-compliance
Lightning Source LLC
Chambersburg PA
CBHW051101230426
43667CB00013B/2397